RIPPING
Gambling
YARNS

*"Live as long as you may,
the first twenty years are
the longest half of your life"*

Robert Southey
Poet Laureate 1813-43

RIPPING *Gambling* YARNS

Michael Church's
Tales of a Misspent Youth

Raceform

Published in 2001 by Raceform Ltd
Compton, Newbury, Berkshire, RG20 6NL.
Raceform Ltd is a wholly-owned subsidiary of MGN Ltd

Copyright © 2001 Michael Church
Line drawings Copyright © 2001 Julia Jacs

A catalogue record for this book is available from the British Library

ISBN   1 901100 68 5

Designed by Phil Brown, Thoroughbred Advertising, London
Printed by The Gresham Press, Old Woking, Surrey

Front cover:–
Top: **Sir Gordon Richards wins the 1953 Derby on Pinza** *(Press Association)*
Bottom left: **Tudor Minstrel (G. Richards up) - winner of the 1947 2,000 Guineas** *(Sport & General)*
Bottom right: **Photo-finish print** *(Author's collection)*
Back cover: **Author, aged 12**

FOREWORD *by Brough Scott*

Every book bar one of this edition needs buying. The remaining one must be kept for the next Time Capsule that is buried in the Woking area. Centuries on, people need to shake their pointed heads/screens in wonder and say – *"surely it cannot have been like this."*

But for Michael Church and all others who loved a punt in the post-war years it was. Unpretentious these stories may be – he likens them to charms on a bracelet – but atmospheric they are to an absolutely magical degree. Life might have been humdrum but betting was an adventure – and illegal to boot.

There is an authenticity here that more famous writers would ache for. When *"Churchy"* invites you in to the betting back room of Charlie Young's Hairdressing Salon you are there in all its smoke-filled wonder. When his infallible greyhound system goes up the spout it hurts right in the solar plexus. And when Sam, his lately-deceased father's Lurcher is elected Woking Football Club's Fan of The Year, it's hard not to wipe away a tear.

When Michael Church first joined us at Racing Post, he was a small stuttering bespectacled accountant with a strange musical laugh which suggested that behind the glasses there was something of a Clark Kent trying to get out. In literary terms that is precisely what happened as he produced his acclaimed series of beautifully presented labours of love on the equine giants of yesteryear.

Now he has switched to his own experiences. They are a long way from the glamour of Ascot and Newmarket but they come in the true quirky voice of a man who knows that hope and laughter are never finally snuffed out until the last betting candle has gone. The best of them will last as true classics of their kind.

And when the *"Pointy Heads"* finally dig up the capsule they will learn that punting memories never die.

CONTENTS

FOREWORD – by Brough Scott   5

INTRODUCTION   10

WHERE DID IT ALL COME FROM? –   13
Eccentric Ancestors

HARRY WRAGG AND THE BRYLCREEM BOY –   18
The Head Waiter's grand finale

GAMES OF SKILL –   24
Cigarette cards and conkers

TUDOR MINSTREL'S YEAR –   30
Seaside holiday, dominated by the Derby

TIN SOLDIER FOOTBALL AND SNAIL RACING –   35
Young entrepreneur promotes after-school activities

BRIGHTON RACES –   40
Saddled with a briefcase

BOXING AND ATHLETICS –   45
Laying the odds on school sports

THE TABLE TENNIS TOURNAMENT –   50
Newcomer threatens handicap fix

CHURCH BROTHERS - FISHMONGERS –   56
Family trip to Wimbledon v Woking

ONE FOR ME - ONE FOR THE SCHOOL –   61
Betting to increase school funds

THE REVENGE COUP –   67
Windsor tips provide pupils' revenge on school bookmaker

WHIST AND WHITE CITY –   72
Big money Whist Drives and Endless Gossip

ACE INFORMATION –   80
Party to a postal tipping scam

A TIP FROM CHARLIE SMIRKE –   85
'What did I Tulyar'

A CORONATION PARTY AND PINZA'S DERBY –   92
Queen Elizabeth and Sir Gordon Richards

GREASE, GREYHOUNDS AND CRIMEWATCH –   98
Involuntary heroics in the RAF
MISS DEECIE TO THE RESCUE –   104
RAF hospital with a full betting service
CHURCHY'S GOLDEN GOOSE –   110
A greyhound system which promised riches
ANOTHER NAIL IN MY COFFIN –   116
Babur wins the Lincolnshire Handicap - twice
GLORIOUS GOODWOOD –   122
A working mens' club outing
THE DEMON KING –   130
Fiddles and fun on a Flapping track
ST PADDY AND ST PETER'S –   136
Derby coup landed after hospitalisation
SHOOTING CRAPS ON THE 8.27 –   141
Commuters' dice game that ends tragically
THE LEVY BOARD EXPERIENCE –   146
Alternative betting in the 'Big Freeze'
LIKE FATHER, LIKE SON? –   151
One man and his dog
RACING POST AND ALL THAT –   157
An epilogue

In the beginning

7

BY THE SAME AUTHOR

- THE DERBY CHART

- THE TWO THOUSAND GUINEAS CHART

- THE MAGNIFICENT SEVEN PEDIGREE CHARTS

- THE GODOLPHIN PEDIGREE CHARTS

- THREE CENTURIES OF LEADING SIRES 1721-1987

- THE CLASSIC PEDIGREE 1776-1989

- DAMS OF CLASSIC WINNERS 1777-1993

- THE DERBY STAKES 1780-1997

- ECLIPSE - The Horse - The Race - The Awards

DEDICATION

R*ipping Gambling Yarns* is dedicated to my wife **Pat**, who has not only helped me to write these yarns, but has keyed in all the contents.

ACKNOWLEDGEMENTS

I t is with much appreciation that I thank **Julia Jacs** for her talented and amusing drawings. Whilst credit is also due to **Graham Rock** for his help with the first and final proofs. Of the staff of *Thoroughbred Advertising*, I should like to thank **Paddy Finlason** for his editing, **Phil Brown** for his design and layout of the book and **Gavin Booker** for the computer programming. Finally, I should like to thank **Martin Stevenson** of *Racing Post* and **James de Wesselow** of *Raceform* for their confidence and support in this project.

INTRODUCTION

R ipping Gambling Yarns is a series of stories strung together like charms on a bracelet – an old car, a dice, a snail, a horse and a dog. And in a way, throughout these, I felt I led a charmed life. Having a stammer was at times a handicap, but my dedication to maths and to the racing pages created countless betting adventures.

Although a kind of personal history, these yarns recall the days before betting shops. To me it seemed a golden age, for my friends at school, my parents, their parents and just about everyone I knew loved a bet.

And, although betting off-course without a credit account was illegal, at every place of work, every public house and in some schools, there was a bookie's runner. Bets were written out on the back of a cigarette packet or a scrap of paper, signed with a code name and wrapped around the money. From time to time, the police raided the collection points but, as often as not, they would also be seen placing a bet when off duty.

It took a while for my obsession to surface for, having narrowly avoided one or two of Hitler's bombs, I was evacuated, as a four-year old, to Llandrindod Wells, a town where gambling was limited to the Christmas raffle and where, on Sundays, pubs were shut and the trains remained stationary. However, on returning home to Woking for our first family reunion on the Sunday before the 1945 Derby, my life was changed irretrievably. It had been nearly five years since our last get-together, but in spite of all the catching up to do, all the talk was of the Derby, and amid the smells of beer and Woodbines, the names of Dante, Midas, Sun Storm, Harry Wragg and Gordon Richards took on a magical appeal. Two of Dad's brothers tried to tell me it was a mug's game, but it was quite useless, for I took to racing like a duck to water, collecting pictures of horses and jockeys for endless scrapbooks. Two years later at the age of 11, I made the decision to set myself up as the school bookmaker.

On leaving school, my first day's work for the Inland Revenue entailed collecting and placing bets at rooms that were raided by the police hours later. My two years' National Service were dominated by horses and greyhounds but, on returning to civvy street, accounts and statistics gradually threaded their way back into my life.

I hope the reader will enjoy the short step back in time, to when betting was daring, fun and often profitable – oh, and to save the now elderly characters portrayed in these yarns from any sleepless nights, I have changed all their names. So let's begin without further ado.

Where did it all come from?

L ooking back, I must have caused my parents many anxious
moments. In my school reports and on Open Days, teachers
would express their concern at my ability to turn anything
competitive into a betting opportunity. On family birthdays and at
Christmas, when relatives visited, they would sometimes point out
to my parents that I must have inherited my obsession for betting
from either this or that side of the family, recalling the exploits of
a some of my relations, and in particular those of my colourful
grandfather, Ernest. As no one had taken the trouble to compile a
family tree, it was from these reunions that I pieced together my
family history.

Around 1900, my father's father Stephen was forced to leave his
position of head groom at a livery stable in the Strand, due to
worsening bouts of asthma. Moving to Woking – then thought of
as the country – he rented a small two-bedroomed, terraced house
in West Street where, with his wife Jane, he raised nine sons and
two daughters. For a few years he made a living by selling
ironmongery, old and new, from the back of a horse and cart in
Steptoe style. But he died suddenly when my father, the youngest,
was two years old, leaving Jane with her eldest sons aged 16 and 17

to keep the family together. Even so, life had its brighter side: my father recalled how on Sunday evenings the whole family would gather round the kitchen table to play Ludo in teams. So much jumping about and banging on the table ensued that his mother would have to keep a firm grip on the oil lamp (their only light) to prevent it being sent flying.

As you can imagine, it was a struggle to survive because there was no Social Security then, but slowly the boys grew up and earned good money as bricklayers, carpenters and painters. Sadly, two of them were killed in the First World War.

Traditionally, the family had always kept an interest in racing and managed to find a shilling or two for a bet on the big races. Later, when the household had half a dozen earners, the bookmaker's runner would call twice a day, and the house would be one of the local centres to hand in a bet. Jane would sit by the back door shelling peas into a colander and enjoying a chat with the punters about the chances of Steve Donoghue or the new boy Gordon Richards.

My mother's side of the family were much better off. They stemmed from Pimlico, where mum's grandfather and his brother made and sold gentlemen's hats, one of which – a straw boater – was purchased by the Prince of Wales. However, her grandfather also suffered from asthma, and he too was advised to live in Woking. A very nervous man, he would sleep with a loaded revolver at the side of his bed.

Mum's mother, Alicia Moore (referred to as Nan in later stories) was the youngest of his seven children and went to an independent school, paying a penny a day. Here she met and fell in love with a local boy, Ernest Barwick, who courted her through school and wrote his proposal of marriage in her history book, which I have to this day. The consummation of their love brought about a hasty marriage and my mother was born two months later.

My grandfather, Ernest, was something of an enigma to both sides

of the family. A sergeant in the First World War, he was later a tele-communications supervisor at Woking Post Office. His extravagant lifestyle always seemed mysteriously superior to his income, which was a constant puzzlement and topic of conversation for the Church brothers who, after a few beers, would make inspired guesses as to the source of his wealth. But no one, as far as I know, ever dared ask him where all his money came from.

His purchase of the first big limousine seen in Woking caused a sensation – three rows of seats, white-wall tyres and long running boards. On many holidays he would transport the whole family, including my mum's sister 'Dutch,' her husband Bob and their terrier 'Binkey,' and on special occasions, I sat alongside him on my Nan's lap and was allowed to sound the horn. Ernest's notoriety grew, for he was reputed to have many mistresses, one of which was always ensconced at our chosen holiday destination.

A keen racegoer, he booked all our holidays near racecourses, and once, outside a hotel in Ayr, two men (bookmaker's heavies) were seen suspiciously loitering around his car. The following morning, while driving off to see his mistress, one of the front wheels came off at a downhill turn. Fortunately he survived, but the immaculate Sunbeam went off the road and would have gone over a cliff had not a sturdy pine tree blocked its path.

Photos of the period show granddad looking like a Mafia patriarch, with striking white curly hair and moustache, splendidly attired in a white suit. Whether Alicia, forever in love with him, was unaware of his philandering, or simply chose to overlook it, was never quite clear. However, the halcyon days inevitably deteriorated, first with a separation from Nan and then finally divorce. Sadly, I never saw him after the age of four, so my memories of him are distant, but by all accounts I was the apple of his eye.

Many years later, a small package addressed to me arrived in the post. It was his gold pocket watch bequeathed to me on his death. The parcel had been despatched from a mental hospital in Wales.

My mother, Dorothy, worked at the Woking Co-op, and some of her father's racing interest must have rubbed off on her as, for many years she would cycle to Royal Ascot, with her work mates, on the Wednesday (early closing). But as a result of her father's philandering, and her mother's silent suffering, she chose to marry Stan, a paragon of caution and reliability. Stanley was a shy, good looking painter and decorator and, unlike most of his brothers, kept regular employment and bought his own house.

So where did it all come from? And why have I always had this obsession for the Derby? Strangely, Dorothy and Stan were married on the day Windsor Lad won the Derby in 1934. And stranger still, my father later told me that I was conceived a year later, on the day Bahram won the great race. Whatever the answer, after a lifetime of study and making the pilgrimage to Epsom, I was overjoyed to receive a commission from *Racing Post* to write the definitive history of the Derby Stakes.

Harry Wragg and the Brylcreem Boy

I knocked twice on the dark stained door at the end of the passage. A small hatch slid open.

"Oxo," I said boldly, standing on tiptoe.

Alice let me in.

"Is the 1.15 off?" I enquired.

"You've got a few minutes yet," she said, dragging on her Woodbine.

I entered the smoke-filled room where the usual crowd huddled around the ticker-tape machine, its stuttering chatter competing with the ringing telephones.

This is the back room of Charlie Young's Hairdressing Salon and, as a chirpy, skinny ten-year-old, my excessive enthusiasm for racing and betting has led me to be accepted by all the regulars. Today is both the last day of the 1946 Flat Season and the last day in the riding career of Harry Wragg, so consequently, my last chance to back him.

Harry was the thinking man's jockey, known nationally as 'The Head Waiter' because of his effective waiting tactics. He had been champion jockey in 1941, and ridden the winners of 13 Classic races, including three Derby winners – Felstead (in 1928), Blenheim (1930) and Watling Street (1942). He also had two younger brothers, Sam and Arthur, who were both successful jockeys in their own right.

Time running out, I quickly scribbled my first bet, *2/- win Tiffin Bell*, (Harry's first mount), and slid it across to Charlie's lankey blonde wife Alice, who promptly secured it among 50 or so others in a giant bull dog clip.

"Two lumps today, Alice," I piped, reaching for the obligatory cup of tea. But before I had put the cup to my lips, Uncle Albert shouted across "Result Manchester – 1.15 – first Tiffin Bell – 5-2.

"Blimey, I'm off to a good start," I squeaked.

During the next 30 minutes, a pipe and two Capstan full strength passed through the security system and quickly contributed to the diminishing visibility.

Continuing my loyalty to H. Wragg, I invested 2/- to win on Aprolon in the next, and made myself useful by taking a tray of tea and biscuits out to Charlie in the shop.

Charlie, a dead ringer for Alfred Hitchcock, often used his ventriloquist talents whilst cutting hair.

"How's it going young squirt?" he enquired, throwing his voice to the corner of the salon.

"I backed Tiffin Bell, won 5-2," I boasted.

"Then you can afford a hair cut he replied," still in the high squeaky voice.

"Sit in the end chair."

"Ten minutes later I re-entered the betting room sporting a well-slicked head.

"Aprolon won at 7-4 Michael," Alice said, coughing manfully, adding, "it must be your lucky day."

"And Harry's," I said.

"What are you doing in the big one?" she enquired.

"Well, I've got to stick to Wragg now, but c-c-can I have a sub on my winnings? I did have a shilling left over, but I had my hair cut."

"Ask Taffy to settle up on one of your slips."

"Bloody hell boyo," said Taffy, "its like looking for a needle in a haystack. Tell you what, I'll lend you two bob until Monday."

"Super," I replied, and instantly returned the coin to his hand.

"Put it on Las Vegas in the N-November Handicap," I stammered.

Two fifteen approached and the request for prices from the ticker-tape had the ring of an auction. Five to one Dornot – Rae Johnson; 100-8 Star of Autumn – Charlie Smirke; 20-1 Las Vegas – Harry Wragg.

Arriving just in time for the big race, I recognised the voices of Uncle Arthur (Craven A), and Uncle Henry (Rothmans), through the blue haze. At this time, it was thought expedient by a health fanatic to take the drastic step of opening a window an inch or two, as visibility had fallen to one pace, and it was difficult to hear the odds over the coughing.

Standing on a chair, Taffy shouted out "Under orders Manchester," shortly followed by "Off Manchester 2-20."

A stillness now came over the assembly, and strangely, the absence of a running commentary in no way diminished the excitement, as each man prepared himself for the instant finality of the result.

The silence was finally broken by the sound of the ticker-tape. Taffy crouched over it assisting its passage like a midwife at a birth.

"Here it comes," Taffy warned ... "Manchester – 2.15 – first, Las Vegas 20-1, second, Delville Wood 33-1, third, Star of Autumn...."

At this point Charlie, burst in shouting "Quiet everybody, quiet, I've just seen two coppers hanging about outside – there's going to be a raid – everyone upstairs, quick as you can."

Charlie then went into his raid-drill: "Alice get rid of the ash-trays, Taffy give me the cash and the books, and put the ticker-tape under the stairs, NOW!"

A crocodile of disgruntled men climbed the stairs to temporarily pay their respects to Alice's bewildered mother, Violet. Meanwhile,

Charlie beckoned to me, "You come with me boy."

"They're at the back door Charlie," Alice cried out.

"Hold them up for as long as you can," he replied, then staring close into the faces of two bemused customers, said, "You've seen nothing, OK – and your haircuts are on the house."

"Michael, put the plank across the arms of that chair, and sit up on it." I obeyed instinctively. Charlie then put the books, cash and betting slips into a pillowcase, pushed it under the plank and threw a large white cape around me to cover everything.

"Afternoon Mr Young." The stentorian voice preceded the presence of two uniformed police officers.

"You've been very busy this afternoon."

"Yes, usual Saturday afternoon you know," Charlie replied, looking a little pale.

"Alice looks as if she has been washing up cups for an army," the sergeant added sarcastically.

"Customers like a cup of tea with their haircut you know."

"Yes of course, we must try that approach down at the station," he retorted.

"Given up the betting, have you Charlie?" he persisted.

"Yes, a mug's game really you know officer."

"You'd be a mug if you got caught Charlie – a heavy fine could close your business down."

"Yes officer, but all that's in the past now," said Charlie, riding his luck.

The sergeant's gaze turned to the customers.

"Been waiting long, gents," he probed, but their nervous mutterings revealed nothing.

Looking in the facing mirror, I watched the copper circle my chair. I could feel my heart beating – my winnings were in that pillowcase.

"This boy's nearly done. Perhaps as a favour you could cut my hair next."

"Crikey," I thought, feeling a rush of blood to my head.

Suddenly, I blurted out, "Ch-Charlie's got to wash it first, officer, I've only just got here."

Charlie's blenched face sprang to life.

"Yes, course I have. His Mum hates all that Brylcreem plastered all over it."

I felt myself propelled forward to the basin for a vigorous hair washing. This having been done under the sergeant's steady gaze,

Charlie was then obliged to begin my second haircut of the afternoon. As the sergeant's puzzled frown deepened, Charlie explained helpfully, "His mum likes it short!"

"Oh well, must be getting along, I suppose." The sergeant slowly moved towards the door before pausing.

"There's just one thing you might like to help with Charlie," he said thoughtfully.

"Of course officer, anything," said Charlie obsequiously.

"I've got ten tickets left for the Police Dance next Saturday, would you like to take them off my hands? Be good for you and Alice to get out occasionally."

Charlie gritted his teeth and paid up.

Leaving by the front door, the two policeman were joined by Uncles Arthur and Henry, tiptoeing down the stairs from the now profoundly bewildered Violet.

"What are you two up to – leaving the scene of the crime?" questioned the sergeant.

"No officer," said Arthur, "we've just been estimating for a wallpapering job."

"A cover up job, more likely."

As the story of this raid went around Woking, so I became the boy hero – albeit with the shortest haircut in Surrey.

Games of Skill

Returning from our evacuation after the war was not the bed of roses we had hoped for. The couple my father had rented our bungalow to had not only left owing three months' rent, but had removed all the internal doors to use as firewood and kept coal in our bath. To cap it all, the agents employed to collect the rent had left town with no forwarding address. But, despite all these inconveniences, we all agreed it was great to be back.

Our first family reunion, the Sunday before the Derby, is recounted in the Introduction and safe to say my interest in betting took off from this point. Two years later, at the age of 11, I started a paper round, and reading *The Sporting Life* and *Greyhound Express* every day fuelled my obsession to the point that I decided to pocket the small bets entrusted to me and pay the winners myself. So, in my first term at the Senior School at Goldsworth, I boldly introduced myself as the school bookmaker.

Sadly my entrepreneurial activities caused me to neglect my schoolwork and, predictably, I failed my 11 plus examination. However, more important to me at the time was the craze for the game of flicking cigarette cards. This entailed two or three boys taking turns to flick them between their first and second fingers against a wall about six foot away. The cards stayed on the floor until a player covered one with another card, at which point he picked them all up.

Down one side of the lower classes playground were two large, covered alcoves for children to shelter under in bad weather. These made ideal pitches for fag card contests, and at playtimes this particular term, there were often three such games taking place simultaneously, with groups of spectators crowding in upon the players.

Most of my friends held a stock of around 100 cards, together with two or three sets given to them in albums by their parents as part of their education. The more skilful players and those with longer arms would let the kitty build up before attempting to cover a card.

As I recall, the most popular sets with the boys were army uniforms, RAF badges, footballers and Derby and Grand National winners. The girls, usually non-players, collected birds, breeds of dogs and butterflies for their aesthetic value. The football set was quite old and rather rare. Uncle Arthur had given me about 30 of these cards the previous Christmas, and during this term I had built up the set until needing only two cards: Stanley Matthews (Stoke) and Cliff Bastin (Arsenal). Both these were scarce because even people who were not collecting the set would keep them for sentiment.

At this time, I had a classroom romance with Laura Mills, a young beauty with blonde, wavy hair and grey green eyes. Coincidentally 'Laura' was the title of the current number one hit on the radio, which I used to my advantage by occasionally serenading her. She was the youngest daughter of a local bank manager, and they were terribly posh, but nevertheless her father collected cigarette cards. During one Friday afternoon, while Laura was watching me play in a contest, she whispered "Look in your desk – there's a present for you." Soon after trooping in for double English Literature, I opened my desk and found a small pink envelope. Inside were Matthews and Bastin, in mint condition. I couldn't believe it. It was beyond my wildest dreams. How did she do it? I had planned to ask her at home-time, but frustratingly I saw her whisked away in a car, leaving me to wait until Monday for the answer.

That weekend I propped up the two precious cards against my bedroom window and, with a warm glow inside, went out and carved Laura's and my initials onto a telegraph pole at the end of our road.

Monday came and, during dinner break, Laura revealed that over the weekend her father had sent the set of footballers (minus two), to a business friend as a goodwill gesture. It seemed he hadn't checked the set. Laura now became anxious on a number of counts: would her father's friend mention the missing cards? If so would her father question her and would she crack under the strain? But more important from my point of view was who would get the blame and it entered my mind that it was no bigger than 9-4 that it would be me.

Haunted by this fear, I was alarmed to be invited to Sunday tea by Laura's mother. As I remember, the jelly and cream buns were delicious, but Laura's parents must have wondered what she saw in a boy who talked relentlessly on obscure subjects, without ever making eye contact or pausing for breath. Mr Mills made a last ditch effort at friendship.

"Laura tells me you're interested in cigarette cards – would you like to see my collection?"

"No thanks," I squeaked.

A long, awkward silence followed. Laura's father gave up and I left shortly afterwards.

Six weeks later, Laura told me she was leaving to go to the Girl's Grammar School, having passed her 11 plus. I can remember eating very little for a day or two and slowly losing my interest in cigarette cards. Fortunately for me, the next craze was about to sweep the school: it was the conker season.

Soon, mums were plagued for meat skewers, balls of string, and of course saucepans filled with vinegar to boil and toughen the best horse chestnuts. This particular conker season was, however, to come to a hitherto unthinkable and abrupt climax. But first let me introduce you to the season's star players – Peter Hapgood and Alfie Parker.

Peter was a short, round, barrel of a boy, in the Billy Bunter mould. Alfie, by comparison, was small, wiley and cunning. Both boys liked a bet, but only when they thought they had an advantage.

For those who have never played the game, each conker has a rating according to the number of conkers it has beaten. And these ratings are accumulative, so if a 2er beats a 3er it becomes a 5er.

One dinner break a championship contest took place between Peter and Alfie to produce a 100er, or, in playground parlance, a 'ton up nut'. To give the contest some bite they had a two-shilling bet on it, asking me to hold the stakes.

The players shaped up within an ever growing circle of onlookers, and since I had studied the form of these conker kings, I chalked up the odds on the wall, 4-6 Peter and 5-4 Alfie. It was quickly observed that Peter had the bigger swing and there was a rush to back him with whatever small change the kids could muster.

Just then, Mr Faraday, a science master on dinner duty, hearing all the shouting and cheering, waded through the crowd.

"What's going on here?"

"It's a conker match sir," I replied, as the outer spectators peeled off.

"I can see that Church, you fool, what's all that money in your cap?"

"Collection for charity, sir."

With that he exploded, confiscating both conkers and all the money.

Since Science was our next period, Faraday, having given me three whacks with the slipper for insolence, had the inspired idea to teach the class some practical physics. I'm afraid I didn't pay full attention to the details of the solutions used at the time but, one conker was covered in something like methylated spirits, while the other was immersed in a sort of resin. Mr Faraday, enjoying his sudden power, proceeded to set light to both conkers. The first glowed like a Christmas pudding, while the second spat and crackled – both filled the laboratory with smoke and fumes.

Alfie was near to tears, while Peter kept croaking 'Bastard' under his breath. Then the unexpected happened, Faraday started poking the conkers with a scalpel and as the fog cleared both literally and figuratively, he asked, "whose conker had the cement core?" keeping a straight face. A moment later, examination of the second conker revealed a band of metal secreted into the nut. Mr Faraday looked up and proclaimed, "Children, we have in our midst a cheat and a fraud." Whereupon the whole class collapsed into laughter. Mr Faraday, hoping to control the ensuing chaos, repeatedly shouted, "Be quiet class, this is a physics lesson," until the bell rang to bring the period to an end. My personal lesson learned was to be more suspicious of high-ranking sporting reputations.

Tudor Minstrel's year

O ne summer holiday of which I have a vivid recollection was in 1947, known in racing circles as 'Tudor Minstrel's year'.

Travelling from Woking to East Wittering by train and taxi, Mum, Dad and I, together with my Grandmother (Nan) and her sister Kate, settled into a smallish bungalow, just off the main road, a few minutes' walk from the sea, shops and the Royal Oak.

Holidays then ran from mid-day Saturday to Saturday, and the last Saturday of our fortnight was Derby Day. This was the first peacetime Derby run on a Saturday and the date, June 7, was therefore not known to my parents at the time of booking, but they were soon made aware of this oversight by my constant protests. For not only would I miss seeing the race, but our return train schedule meant I would also, in those pre-transistor days, be unable to hear the radio commentary.

Nevertheless, every morning I would get up early to walk our terrier Judy to the newsagent's for the papers. Back at the bungalow, I would cut out all the news and photographs of the Derby horses, in particular from the *Daily Graphic*, which had a photograph and form guide to a different Derby contender every day. These I pasted into a scrapbook with loving care.

Around this time it seemed almost everyone had a shilling each-way on their fancy in the Derby. But since betting was then illegal, unless on the course or with a credit account, our family and everyone we knew placed their bets through an assortment of bookies' runners, milkmen, hairdressers and publicans.

Gordon Richards, then the perennial champion jockey, had ridden the winners of every Classic race except the Derby. Having continually chosen the 'wrong horse' when his retaining stable had more than one runner, he was thought by the superstitious to have a Derby jinx. This year however, was deemed to be 'Gordon's year', for his Derby mount was the brilliant Tudor Minstrel. Top of the Free Handicap the previous season, Tudor Minstrel had recently won the Two Thousand Guineas in a canter by eight lengths from Saravan and Sayajirao.

Earlier that year, as a newspaper boy, I remembered the headlines *'Horse of the Century,'* with further superlatives written around photographs of Tudor Minstrel and arrows pointing to various parts of his anatomy.

Now certain to start at odds-on for the Derby, stories abounded about punters who had waded in to win fortunes on him before the Guineas. And such was the charisma that surrounded the horse and the Derby of that year, that 30 years later, after having my appendix removed, the man in the next hospital bed told me that he had taken 7-1 to a week's wages about the horse, more than a year before the event.

All this hype however, had made very little impression on Aunty Kate, who insisted that Saravan would turn the tables on Gordon. Mum liked to back a grey, so chose Migoli, while Dad followed the Australian jockey Edgar Britt and hoped Sayajirao would win. Nan fancied the Irish horse Grand Weather, on the grounds it had been the hottest week of the year, with people frying eggs on the pavement! It was also decided that the dog should not be left out of the excitement and Merry Quip was chosen to be her runner. As we would not be back in time to get our bets on with our local hairdresser, a shilling sweep was arranged. But due to the considered reasoning that had gone into our selections, everyone wanted to keep the horse they had chosen, rather than risk the hazards of an orthodox sweep. And in view of my protest at missing the race, I was allowed to have Tudor Minstrel, but I had to put in the dog's shilling to level up the odds.

The holiday continued in the usual fashion, including trips to the beach where I played French cricket, made sandcastles and splashed about in a car-tyre's inner tube as, despite the patient efforts of my father, I never learned to swim. Returning to the bungalow in the evening, Mum and Nan would cook up some beans on toast, followed by tea and cakes. Dad and I would wash up and, later, a green baize cloth would be thrown over the table for a game of cards or dominoes. Cards were a particular feature of our family evenings, with games such as Whist or Solo and, if there were more than four players, Switch, Newmarket, Race the Ace, Pontoon and Banker. These games were always played for small amounts of money to keep the interest alive. On this and some other holidays, Auntie Mary, Uncle Henry and Cousin Peter would arrive for the day but stay over-night, sleeping on settees and in arm-chairs, to return the following morning. But always, there would be cards in the evening.

One morning, Auntie Mary, seeing me pasting cuttings into my scrapbook, asked me who I thought would win the Derby and, on hearing of our sweep, wanted shilling tickets for herself, Henry and Peter. However, on learning that all the fancied horses had already been taken, she had to be persuaded into taking two outsiders for the price of one. She chose the two streets, Tite Street and Castle Street, ahead of Henry who picked two French horses, Cadir and Parisian. Henry had always wanted to go to Paris and, as he was on holiday, thought it a lucky omen.

When Peter, (aged seven), came in from the garden, he was asked to pick two horses from the remaining five.

"I'll have Firemaster, 'cos I pass the Firestation on the way to school. And has Merry Quip gone?" he chirped.

"Has it?" enquired Mary.

"Yes," I said, "we picked that one for the dog."

"Can you change it?" Mary asked anxiously.

"Not really," I said, "we've written it down now and we don't want to disappoint her."

Peter, a stubborn little blighter, wouldn't budge, for apart from liking the name, he had been told at school that Tommy Weston, the jockey, had great faith in the horse. To avoid tears, a compromise was

agreed – Peter was to pay sixpence and share Merry Quip with the dog. Further discussions went on when it was known that I had already paid the dog's stake, but no refunds were made.

As the holiday came to an end, so Derby Day loomed nearer. The cases were packed, Judy given her last walk and the sea was said goodbye to for another year. On the train journey home, no one spoke of the Derby. But from 2.30 onwards, I began checking the time at ten-minute intervals, imagining first the saddling up, the paddock scene, and then the parade, followed by the canter to the start. As the train pulled into Guildford Station I knew the race was over. I now dreaded overhearing the winner's name from a passenger's casual conversation.

On arriving at Woking Station, we took a short taxi ride home. Without any explanation from me or comment from my parents, I asked to be dropped off at Charlie Young's Hairdresser's Shop at the corner of our road.

Pushing into the smoke filled back-room where all the bets were taken, I blurted out to Charlie's wife: "Who won the Derby?"

"A French long-shot, Pearl Diver, 40-1," came the reply.

"Second and third," I squeaked.

"Migoli and Saya-watsit," she responded.

"What happened to Gordon?"

"Led at Tattenham but didn't stay; finished fourth. Charlie won a packet on the race – says there's a jinx on Richards in the Derby!"

Footnote

For those who like a tidy finish, the sweep, not won, (Pearl Diver was the only horse under 200-1 that we hadn't picked), was carried forward to the following year, when Nan picked and backed the Aga Khan's My Love at 100-8. As for my torture of missing the Derby, this tragedy only recurred twice in the next 53 years.

Tin Soldier Football and Snail Racing

Soldier Football was a game that my father and I had derived from various other football games. It was played with two teams of 11 lead or tin soldiers, on a rug about four feet by three. The goals, in proportion, were made of wood, supported and covered at the back with a hair-net. The lines were drawn with chalk, a small marble used for the ball and the players were in fixed positions.

The game was strictly a passing game: when you kicked-off, if the ball was not closer to your player, the opposition played it. You could shoot from anywhere, but only the goalkeeper could be moved along his goal line.

Dad and I spent many winter evenings playing out games between teams with assumed names such as "Carpathians" and "Wizard Wanderers." Soldiers striking war-like postures or Indian braves running looked better and were often more useful than, say, a guardsman standing to attention or a military trombone player. We soon assessed which particular soldiers were best shaped for certain positions and these 'regulars' were bound around in wool in the team's colours and coloured shorts were sewn on.

Eventually, after discussing the game with Bill Long, my games master, I was asked to give the class a demonstration one wet day when the school's soccer pitch was waterlogged.

The game was to be played between the two best footballers in the class – Roy 'Dixie' Dean, a forceful striker who went on to be a taxi-driver, and Martin Crawford, a thoughtful defender who became a house-agent. I stood on the 'touch lines' explaining the rules, while Mr Long kept order between the players and the partisan class, who gathered round shouting support for 'their man'. Fifteen minutes each-way with added time for disputes, aptly filled the 45 minutes of time allowed. The final score of 6-5 to Dean brought much excitement and Dixie became a hero for the day.

There was some betting on the game but, being the referee, I could not be seen taking bets. Instead, my clerk, Colin Nixon, laid an even half-a-crown on Dixie, but covered by laying 3-1 the draw. There was much talk of a return match, but the noise generated by the game, plus the distinct possibility of betting, caused the Headmaster, Mr 'Bonk' Peel, to forbid it.

Due to the general enthusiasm for the game, five of the boys and myself formed a league and played games, home and away, in our houses. The five home games at my house after school drew added interest since, during an extended half-time interval, two snail races were run.

The day before the match, snails were gathered from dad's cabbage patch and their shells painted in watercolours in the racing silks of the day. Anyone who attended the match could pick a snail, put sixpence in the kitty, and the winner took all. Allowing the visitors the courtesy of first choice of snail did not, however, give them any great advantage. The chances of them selecting the snail I had previously observed as the liveliest were remote, and even if they did, I could lay some of the other snails at bigger prices.

The course was a garden seat made from a level plank of wood about five feet long and nine inches wide. Painted green and wiped over with a damp cloth, it was to be the focus of our attention. The snails were kept on a few lettuce leaves in an old colander, and when selected, were lined up at one end of the seat. After the draw – important not to get the extreme inside or out, in case your snail disappeared over the side – some small wagers were struck. These were win only, since waiting for the second and third snail to cross the line had in the past caused some aggravation. Brian Smith, the son of a famous local footballer, had refused to start the second half of the football match until the third snail had crossed the line, so causing the game to be abandoned when his father arrived with a torch.

At the end of our soldier-football season it was decided to have a knock-out cup, and by adding Bobby and Billy Powell, the two boys next door, we made up a total of eight teams, so avoiding the process of byes. My father, keen on the event, provided a small silver plated cup (which he had won when playing football for Pyrford) for the winner, and Mum had promised to make sandwiches for the spectators.

Bobby and Billy had been given a football set of 'soldiers' at Christmas, one team in Arsenal colours and the other in Wycombe Wanderers' – an interesting choice at the time as Wycombe (light and dark blue quarters), were in the Isthmian League with Woking.

The first round draw was made in the school playground one lunch-time. It was decided that Peter Hopgood, a small fat boy with a loud voice, would make the draw from his cap. Slowly, the pieces of paper were withdrawn. However, Peter's loud voice and the intermittent cheers, as someone welcomed a home draw, had attracted a crowd of boys, and also the attention of Headmaster 'Bonk' who, scattering the crowd, requested the presence of Peter and me in his study immediately. Our explanations that it was only a draw for a soldier-football knockout cup, did not, however, allay his fears that this was yet another vehicle for betting. Consequently threats of three strokes of the cane were made if he saw any money change hands. Strangely enough, he always allowed me to have Derby Day off and usually asked me to put a bet on for him.

The cup-final was played between Bobby Powell and my cousin Peter – the two youngest players in the competition and both complete outsiders in the betting. Despite my efforts for the rounds to proceed as in the real F.A.Cup, some of the boys went on family holidays and one contestant was confined with chicken-pox. The final was a friendly affair, with Bobby's parents in support and Auntie Mary

(Peter's mother) coming over for a chat with Mum. Bobby, using his Arsenal set of players, led 2-0 half-time. But during the interval, Peter, a shy but determined lad, wound countless layers of wool around his full backs, and in particular his goalkeeper, a soldier in the position of a hand-grenade thrower, with arms wide apart. The result was a critical narrowing of the goal mouth.

On resumption of play, Bobby didn't notice Peter's swollen defenders, but his father did. However, since his son was winning 2-0 he kept silent. A few minutes from the end of the game, two things happened. First, Peter scored a goal from a long kick taken from his own half and then the fire siren went. Bobby's father was a fireman and the Fire Station in Woking was less than 100 yards from his house, so he jumped on his bike and rode off at great speed.

Owing to the interruption, a further two minutes were added to play. Surprisingly, Peter scored from a deflection after a corner; two-two. With fears of objections from Bobby's father about the extra wool-winding, and Auntie Mary's embarrassed apologies for her son's skulduggery, it was agreed that no extra time should be played, but that each player should keep the cup for six months.

The next day, I heard my father and Mr Powell discussing the match over our garden fence. Mr Powell was being rather self-righteous about under-age betting and Dad, as usual, was being the peacemaker. Soon after, the cup was handed back and allegedly sent for engraving but was never seen again. Evening snail race meetings, however, continued to flourish.

Brighton Races

I had recently seen *'Brighton Rock'*, the film of Graham Greene's classic crime thriller, where a young Richard Attenborough plays 'Pinkie', the leader of a razor gang, working a bookmaker protection racket at Brighton races. And although this era was at an end, the film had given the racecourse a popular notoriety that added a buzz to the meetings.

On learning that a race meeting at Brighton coincided with our family holiday, I persuaded my father to take me, and it proved a day to remember for this impressionable 13-year-old. To begin with, I spotted Billy Cook, the Australian champion jockey, walking towards us at the back of the stands. Hastily producing a racecard and pen, I asked him for his autograph. Cook, who had been in England for about three months, already had the tinge of a London accent, and his gaunt face and heavy eyebrows belied his pleasant manner. Plucking up courage I said, "Are you riding anything good today Billy?"

"Well I've only got two rides; the one in the first is a long shot, but my ride in the last has a chance."

"Last race Cook, eh?" I replied, for this was what Fleet Street had dubbed him after a recent run of last race successes.

Getting into racecourses was quite expensive in those days, and Dad paid an uncomfortable amount to get into Tattersalls, followed by a small contribution to the Gateman to look the other way as I scrambled over the turnstile.

Once inside, we found our bearings and marked our selections in the racecard. It was a bright sunny day, and the smell of the freshly cut grass, together with the sight of the shimmering heat-haze over the course, and the sound of horses hooves pounding to post created a sudden assault on my boyhood senses which crystallised into a lasting memory.

Neither Dad nor I had a bet in the first race, and Billy Cook's long shot finished well down the field. But running in the next was National Spirit, a long time favourite of mine, who, trained by Vic Smyth at Epsom, had twice won the Champion Hurdle. I made him my 'Nap of the Day,' and, having obtained evens to a pound note, our cheers were drowned in the deafening roar as the old fella drew away coming up the hill.

Just after Dad had collected our winnings, an incident occurred that changed our day. Frank Rogers, one of Uncle Albert's shadier friends, appeared hurrying towards us.

"Are you staying for the last, Stan?" he anxiously enquired.

"Yes it's a lovely day isn't it," said Dad.

"Would you do me a great favour and look after my briefcase?"

Dad hesitated. "It will get me out of a spot," Frank added.

"OK, but where will we meet you?" Dad cautiously enquired.

"Up there at the back of the stand," Frank said pointing, "after the weigh-in."

As the runners were leaving the Paddock for the next – the Brighton Mile – I persuaded Dad to go halves on Star Signal in the first leg of a Tote Double, while I looked after Frank's case. Once again we had something to shout about, as Star Signal won in a canter, while Dad resumed control of the briefcase.

Finding a place to sit while enjoying our tea and sticky buns, we began to question why Frank had trusted us with his briefcase and why he looked so anxious about it. After the second sticky bun, I could no longer contain my curiosity.

"Come on Dad, let's have a quick look inside."

"Its probably locked," he replied.

"It isn't Dad, I've just tried it."

"Well, OK then," Dad said with uncharacteristic abandon, "just a quick look."

I flicked the case open ... "Bloody hell!"... and shut it smartly. It was full of bundles and bundles of pound notes. Just then, the loudspeakers announced the overweights for the next race and Dad scuttled off unsteadily to bet a few shillings on the Tote, leaving me to clasp the briefcase tightly with sweaty hands.

In stark contrast to the contents of the case, Dad's place on the Tote paid 4/3d (21p). And even then it took us a minute or two to sort out the right ticket, since, in those days, they had to be held up to the light to read a series of perforations that revealed not only the number of the horse and race, but also a four letter code-word. This persistent scrutiny tested the patience of both the punters and cashiers alike, and continually caused lengthy, slow moving queues at the pay-out windows.

Exchanging our Daily Double ticket for the second leg, we both agreed to plump for the Duchess of Norfolk's Suivi, the long odds-on favourite, and, after checking the safety of the briefcase for the tenth-time, Dad was able to relax in time to see the horse skate home by four lengths.

It was now time for the last race and, remembering to back Billy

Cook, we opted to bet with the bookies, as the Tote queues continued to grow. The bet on, Dad and I stood high in the stand to watch the race and wait for Frank. Cook was riding Dorothy Paget's Wynola, and we watched her famous blue, with yellow hoop colours glide gracefully to the start.

The best price available was 13-8 but, having bumped into Billy at the start of the day, we felt duty bound to back it.

A furlong out, the roar of the crowd told the story as Cook cruised into the lead to win easily, and whilst by our standards we had had a stunningly successful day's racing, the presence of Frank's briefcase put our profit into perspective. We were just beginning to worry about him, when he suddenly turned up at our side.

"Thanks for looking after the case Stan. Saved my day. Have to dash now I'm afraid."

And with that, he took the case, looking back to say "Must buy you a drink next time."

For a moment we stood there stunned, until Dad said, "Thank heavens for that, I thought we were going to get stuck with all that money."

Suddenly, we remembered we hadn't collected our winnings, so in a bit of a panic, Dad gave me the bookie's ticket to collect, while he went off to cash our Daily Double.

I caught up with him at the back of the Tote queue.

"One pound sixteen shillings between us," he said.

"Oh well, it could be worse," I replied, "but I'd have rather hung on to the briefcase!" And part of me meant it.

Flashbacks of the inside of that case haunted me for many months to come.

Boxing and Athletics

These were the days of heroes, and at most Secondary Modern Schools of the time, they constituted either the school cricket or football captains, athletes or boxers – but never brainy kids or swots, and never, ever, school bookmakers, however young.

Here are a couple of events in the school's year that brought two such heroes into direct confrontation.

Fighting in the playground at Goldsworth School was now a regular occurrence and the parents of Sandals Smith and Nipper Lynch had already seen the headmaster about their sons being bullied. One morning at Assembly, the Deputy Headmaster Bill Long, made an announcement that, in future, P.T. (Physical Training) lessons would include the art of boxing. Bill had been a successful high jumper in the Army and retained all his military bearing, tall and upright with a ginger moustache: he was not a man to mess with.

The gloves duly arrived and, so as not to disrupt the school, the teaching of the 'Noble Art' was performed in one of the annexed huts used by the A.T.C. (Air Training Corps). My one and only pugilistic encounter confirmed my worst fears – that when hit smartly on the nose, stars could clearly be seen. This convinced me that my role as school bookmaker had been wisely chosen. Almost every boy boxed a bout at some time or another and, as a trial for an Open Day Exhibition Match, the school's two best potential heavyweights, Eddie Silver and Peter Kay, were asked to box for four one-minute rounds.

It is hard to imagine the excitement the fight generated. Eddie came from a sporting family and, at 15, already had the face of a boxer. Peter, by comparison, had a refined appearance. He was then Head Boy and also held the school record for the mile. Entering into the spirit, their respective form teachers gave them time off for training, and neither boy was questioned on going back for 'seconds' at school dinners. I also entered into the spirit of the event by offering odds of 4-6 Silver and evens Kay. Hwfa Jones, the Maths Master, grudgingly conceded I'd got it about right. Sixpences and shillings poured in, equally divided between the two contestants, although the girls generally favoured Kay and asked for receipts.

At last, the big day came. A square was chalked out six paces by six, in a shady area of the playground (the school never could afford a proper ring), and benches were put around all sides of the square for a few spectators. The time of the fight was arranged to coincide with the regular lessons but, as I recall, faces were pressed against the woodwork room windows and a steady flow of pupils visited the outside toilets. Mysteriously, by the time the boxers touched gloves, there were well over 100 spectators.

Soon the boxers were staring into each other's eyes, shuffling from one foot to the other. The bell rang and both came to the centre of the ring, bobbing and weaving in contrasting styles. Kay had the appearance of a slightly manic kangaroo drumming a punchbag, while Silver moved his head from side to side like a snake, emitting threatening snorts while banging his gloves together. But despite this elaborate posturing, at the end of the first round neither boxer had thrown a single punch.

A fervent inter-round encouragement by Long brought both boxers up for round two, but after some dedicated pushing, shoving and holding, still no punches were thrown. At this point, questions began to form in the minds of the onlookers ... were the boxers giving each other too much respect? Were they terrified of each other? Or had someone fixed the fight? Halfway through the third round, Bill Long, now exasperated beyond endurance, sent both boxers back to their corners and stopped the contest. After a stunned silence, jeers, scuffles and small fights broke out in the crowd. In a last ditch attempt to avoid refunding all the stakes, I called out to Mr Long, "Are you giving the result a draw sir?"

"No," he said, "You haven't been betting on this have you Church?"

I melted away with the crowd.

The abrupt curtailment of this potential money-spinner did not leave me down-hearted for too long, for School Sports Day, with its myriad possibilities, was looming.

Athletics, and in particular running, was very popular at school and everyone was expected to enter at least one event. Heats were run off the week before, so that on the day only the semi-finals and finals of each event took place before the assembled school and parents. Naturally there was betting, with most of the money taken on the day. The 440 yards was usually the most open race, since it attracted both sprinters and stayers, eager to gain more points for their House.

Our school, although not owning their own sportsground, were privileged to use the facilities at Horsell, a large ground at which Surrey County Cricket Club came to play a one-day exhibition game every year. Completely surrounded by a high hedge, it had a smart pavilion at the entrance, from which the prizes were presented at the end of the day.

The 440 yards this year had two semi-finals with eight runners in each. Together with my clerk Colin Nixon, I issued prices on the

morning for the final – win only; bets to be made before the first semi-final – all in, run or not. This gave us a chance of laying the more fancied runners at better prices. As I remember, Peter Kay and Silver were 3-1 joint favourites, with Martin Crawford and Dixie Dean, both school soccer players, on 7-1. Colin and I had got through the heats, but neither of us had a prayer and the 20-1 we offered about us was far from generous. Almost all the money taken was for the first four favourites so any chance of a profit looked slim.

Our first bit of luck came when Dixie pulled a muscle after winning a sprint semi-final. And it continued, when Crawford was cruelly spiked in the other semi. However, when Kay and Silver both won their 440 semi's with a bit in hand, we still looked on a hiding to nothing.

Twenty minutes later, Eddie Silver and I lined up for the 220 semi's. Eddie, knowing that the quarter-mile final would quickly follow, did just enough to qualify, whereas I tried to win it, and was beaten a yard in an all-out finish.

On returning to the pavilion, Eddie and I were marshalled straight to the start of the 440 final, where my breathless protests went unheeded. Lining up, not in lanes, but on the outside with Eddie as seven and me as eight, my chance seemed less than hopeless. Thinking quickly, I seized the opportunity for a moment's glory, going straight to the front and leading until the third bend, where I promptly blacked out and fell, bringing down Peter Kay, who in turn caused Silver to stumble. As fate would have it, I had eliminated the two hot favourites at a stroke. Colin Nixon, wide of the trouble, saw his opportunity and ran on to unexpected glory. The first-aiders, followed by the Red Cross, were swiftly on the scene and I remembered being carried back on a brown canvas stretcher to the pavilion.

Later that afternoon, the prizes were given out amid cheers all around, with Nixon receiving his medal, still in stunned amazmnt. Although there were some disgruntled rumblings from the more committed punters, and the connections of Kay and Silver, this sports day was generally considered a great success by the school. Looking at our betting ledger, Colin and I were in complete agreement.

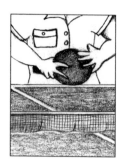

The Table Tennis Tournament

Following the Festival of Britain, the 1950's were anticipated as an age of enlightenment with unsurpassed student opportunities in education. Very little of this, however, impinged on Goldsworth Secondary Modern. Except in one case.

The senior teachers, full of the new 'Elizabethan spirit', were concerned that the boys and girls of the fourth and fifth forms should integrate more for social activities. So they bought two table tennis tables, to be used after lessons and on wet days, as an alternative to outdoor games. At this time my class was blessed with a young 'relief teacher', Mr Parrot, who, since covering maths and games, was given the task of drawing up a rota/timetable, so that pupils knew who and when they were playing. To begin with, the proceedings appeared to be highly organised, but after a few evenings people started dropping out and the waning interest gave Mr Parrot cause for concern. It seemed that most of the girls didn't like playing the boys and vice versa, as the games were often one sided and occasionally resulted in intimidation, rather than friendship.

Mr Parrot, who by now had become either Pretty Polly, Pollyanna or, to those more mathematically inclined, Polygon, decided on a system of giving each player a handicap to level up the matches and create a more competitive interest. When Colin Nixon and I were told about this, we looked at each other open mouthed – it was like manna from heaven!

The following day, I suggested to Polly that we held an end of term knock out competition like the F.A. Cup, with perhaps a trophy for the best boy and best girl.

"A capital idea Church," he responded.

"You're a maths man – perhaps you would keep tabs on it. And if you are going to be around after school, let me know if any of the handicaps need adjusting."

That evening Colin and I thought long and hard, and although we both had a lot of homework to do, we just watched the table tennis and made a few notes on the players and their handicap marks. After a few evenings we agreed that our strategy had to be slow and easy. Any signs of betting and ante-post lists would send out alarm signals to Polly and spoil an end-of-term coup. Then I came up with the solution. We wouldn't run a book on it at all, but would suggest to Brian Fisher, (another aspiring bookmaker), that at the end of term he run a book on it, thereby allowing us to compete. Our plan, of course, was to lose by a few more points than necessary against good players, so that our handicaps would slowly go up. No one would be suspicious, because there would be no betting, at least until the end of term. Colin and I grinned our way through double-scripture until our teacher, Ma Snow, referred to us as the 'Cheshire cats'.

As weeks rolled by, Colin and I steadily increased our handicaps by careful play, and in some instances it took a great deal of skill to lose convincingly to poorer players. Equally important, we contrived to reduce the handicaps of the better players. Although Fisher had watched the table tennis and even played a few games, he had not seen either Colin or I surreptitiously throw away the few odd points. The result was, at the end of term, when 31 names and a bye went into the hat for the first round, Fisher went 8-1 the field, with Colin and I both on 100-8. The whole thing looked like a dream scenario: Colin and I had effectively a four point better start than our true form in a first-to-21 point game, while the final was to be the best of three.

Peter Kay, Dixie Dean and Eddie Silver were all between eight and ten to one, and backed themselves and each other for a few shillings. But there was little money for any of the girls excepting Janet O'Brien and Jackie Spencer, who both excelled at sports.

"Come on Churchy, aren't you having a bet," urged Fisher.

"OK," I replied with studied unconcern, "just for a bit of fun then. I'll have four shillings to win 50 on Colin and the same on myself."

"And how about you Colin," he enquired.

"I'll have the same if it's OK with you Brian?"

"Blimey, it's a good job I've got some cash in already, otherwise I couldn't stand it."

After our bets were pencilled in, some of the un-backed players were pushed out to 33-1 to attract a steady flow of sixpences and shillings, so rounding up Fisher's book.

Two days before the first round matches, there was a buzz of betting fever going around the fourth and fifth forms with Brian in the midst of it. And although Polly had been warned about Brian's book, he had decided to overlook the matter.

The following morning, Headmaster 'Bonk' Peel closed assembly with the announcement that a new boy, Henry Beauchamp, would be joining the school next term and would be sitting in with the fourth form for the last two weeks to meet his fellow pupils. It seemed his father was an influential man and had persuaded Peel it would be good for the boy. Later that day, Polly dropped the bombshell that Henry Beauchamp had taken the place of the 'bye'

in the draw and was to play Janet O'Brien in the opening game on the following day.

"What's he like?" enquired Colin.

"Not bad apparently; he played for the YMCA Juniors in Richmond," replied Polly, "but I've given him the same handicap as you and Church to be diplomatic."

Immediately our smugness turned to panic. Brian, of course, was delighted with having an un-backed favourite in his book and cautiously chalked up Beauchamp at 4-1. News of Beauchamp's prowess travelled fast as punters rushed to cover their bets, but, after the new boy put Janet away 21-8, Brian drastically reduced his price to 2-1.

Round followed round with sometimes as many as 40 pupils staying behind to cheer on their favourites. And although our homework fell hopelessly behind, it was apparent that the teachers had achieved the social integration they were looking for.

In the semi-finals, Colin and I, having won a few laid-back games, were drawn against each other, but since we had the same bets, it didn't matter too much who won. Henry Beauchamp, who continued to attract financial support as many of the original favourites were eliminated, was drawn against the last girl left in, Jackie Spencer. Henry's semi came first, and, receiving two points, he won 21-13, with his father giving much vocal support. In the other semi-final I just managed to beat Colin 21-19, after an unusually skilful and energetic game.

The final was played on the evening before the last day of term. It was to be the best of three games and for once I received some vocal support. For although Beauchamp was well backed, he was at this point regarded as an intruder. Once again his father was present, this time at the side of the Headmaster.

The handicaps worked out level for this match and Beauchamp

took the first game 21-17, after I twice had a point deducted for cupping the ball in my hand on serving, rather than keeping my palm flat. In the second game, Beauchamp led 12-8, as I had yet another two points taken away for foul serves. At this change of service, Beauchamp asked the referee, Mr Parrot, if he could obtain from his father his asthma tablets and a glass of water. This caused some disquiet among the onlookers, but play was resumed some five minutes later. It was now my turn to serve, and, after further persuasion from Polly about the open palm, I took the next five points. Through all this Henry Beauchamp suddenly seemed to lose concentration and I won the second game 21-18.

A tense atmosphere surrounded the third game. I led 11-9 at the halfway stage and upon the change of service Beauchamp's father called out to his son to take deep breaths. As I edged further ahead, Mr Beauchamp's voice rang out: "Get a grip on yourself Henry." At this point, Headmaster 'Bonk' found an excuse to swiftly leave the Hall. A few minutes later Polly announced, "Church wins by two games to one, 17-21, 21-18 and 21-15." I can remember some cheering and Brian Fisher later shouting "pieces of eight," when paying out Colin and I, almost under the nose of Polly.

Sadly, there were no trophy presentations and we later heard that Peel had wanted to see how the first competition went before splashing out on silver. Next day, the match, and Bonk's stingyness, were the talk of the school, while Colin and I happily agreed with Mr Parrot what a wonderful thing this age of enlightenment was, with its 'unsurpassed student opportunities'.

Church Brothers – Fishmongers

Christmas is a time for families, and so it was with us. Dad was the youngest of 11 children and all nine boys played football for local teams and followed Woking F.C. throughout their lives.

On Boxing Day, Dad's brother Albert, who sold wet fish from the back of his small van (the only vehicle in our extended family), decided to treat his brothers by taking them to Woking's away match at Wimbledon. Both teams then played in the Isthmian League – the top flight of amateur football.

Albert duly scrubbed out the van with carbolic, while brother Charlie, a bricklayer, acquired planks and bricks to construct two bench seats in the back. As I remember, ten of us made the trip, Albert and his son John were in the front seats, while the brothers Charlie, George, Ernie, Arthur, Henry, cousin Peter, Stan (Dad) and I squeezed into the back.

Boxing Day arrived with a light fog, and the brothers, complete with vacuum flasks of tea and Oxo tins filled with turkey sandwiches, piled into the van. Almost immediately, we knew it was a journey to endure. At every bend, we had to steady ourselves by clutching the man opposite tightly, and, to contact Albert, we had to bang on the boards that separated us from the driver's cabin.

Dad and I, being the last in, had the advantage of looking out of the tiny oval windows in the back doors, but, by the time we had reached Weybridge (half-way), we all felt a little queasy and Henry's efforts to pass around cups of tea from his flask only resulted in scalded hands, wet knees and cries of "Bugger it!"

Approaching Walton-on-Thames, those with the weakest bladders were banging on the back of the cabin in desperation, shouting for Albert to pull over. On disembarking, we could see the fog had thickened up, but Charlie said it would be all right if the referee could see both goals from the half-way line, which gave us hope. Cousin Peter seemed more concerned in keeping the crease sharp in his first pair of long trousers, a Christmas present which promised to increase his credibility among his schoolmates. Albert, on the other hand, was worried about Kempton races being off. It was, of course, King George Day. All the brothers loved a bet, but none more than Albert, who spent all his time dreaming up systems, without a shred of logic to any of them. On this day he was backing horses that were pulled up last time out!

Suitably relieved, we all scrambled back into the van and journeyed on, clutching each other on the bends, until finally we arrived at Plough Lane – home of Wimbledon F.C. In those days very few people owned a car, so parking close to the ground was easy. But ten people emerging into the light from a small fish van drew some attention, particularly as we continued to shout at each other at the volume which had been necessary to cover the engine noise.

Delighted that the fog had lifted, we gathered ourselves, adjusted our volume and made for the entrance. After clicking through the turnstiles, we bought our programmes and took up positions behind the goal at the Durnsford Road end.

Each of the Church brothers had their own distinct way of

showing their involvement in the game. Dad would jump up for the corners, elbow the man next to him in a shoulder charge and often cleared the line with a wild forward kick. All of this was tolerated by those related to him, but most other supporters moved well away, leaving him a clear space either side. Once, at Woking, he was reputed to have elbowed my mother smartly off

her seat and into the aisle. Brother Arthur, an ex-sergeant, was given to military outbursts, such as "Cut through their left flank and let'um have it," whereas the only signs of emotion from Henry was a facial twitch and, when under extreme pressure, the lighting of two cigarettes simultaneously. His son, Peter (the youngest Church), had been known to squeak continuously for up to five minutes at moments of high excitement. Naturally, I was ever watchful for opportunities to lay the brothers tempting prices about penalties or the next goal scorer.

Five minutes before the kick-off, although a large crowd had packed into the ground, we still had ample room around us. A nearby fan solved this mystery by complaining loudly about the smell of kippers. Apparently, Albert's diligent van cleaning had not been enough, and we were all enveloped in a fishy aroma. By the time the brothers recognised it and had told each other, the teams were running out on the pitch.

John and I had home-made rosettes and large wooden rattles, which we would whirl over our heads to produce ear-splitting machine gun sounds. This we did wildly in the first half as, to our delight, Woking scored twice. The stunned Dons supporters blamed their players' woeful performance on their Christmas excesses.

The second half had resumed a full 20 minutes before Henry noticed that young Peter had not returned from the toilets, and it was not until Woking went 3-0 up, that John and I could be persuaded to go and ferret him out. After checking the gents we began asking the Stewards if they had seen a small boy with curly hair, glasses, a Woking scarf and well creased trousers. This was by no means the first time Peter had gone missing at a sporting event. At Ramsgate dogs, we found him up a ladder inside the Tote indicator board, and later at Goodwood, he was eventually spotted sharing another family's picnic.

Eventually, John and I returned to watch the game Peterless, but not unduly concerned, and it was not until the final whistle that he appeared, tear stained, at Henry's side.

"Sorry Dad, I slipped over in the gents, soaked my new trousers and broke my glasses. But a kind lady looked after me and bought me lots of chips."

Henry's anger was tinged with relief, first with having his son back, and secondly with the final whistle. Three-nil to Woking, with goals by Alfie Zimmer, Charlie Mortimer and Freddie Pink, and another clean sheet for Phil Ledger.

For those concerned, Peter dried off nicely on the journey home.

Later, when dropping off everyone outside Woking Railway Station, Albert bought an evening paper.

"How did yer horses get on?" we enquired.

"No good – not even placed," replied Albert, smiling bravely. "Never mind," he brightened, "I've done a great deal on some smoked haddock coming in Tuesday, so perhaps you'll all buy some – special family rates, of course."

ANY DOUBLE
2-1

One for Me – One for the School

Throughout my second and third year in the Senior School, the teaching staff were constantly questioning my motivation. And, had Timeform assessed my school work, they would no doubt have marked me with both a letter P (likely to make more than normal progress, and their notorious squiggle (cannot be relied upon). However, at the beginning of term in the fourth year, I received a gift from the Gods which changed everything.

When the Maths text-books were passed around, by some twist of fate, I was given the tutor's version containing the answers, and by another twist of fate, my teacher, Bill Long, never missed it. Now this was exciting. After a moment's thought, my future was clear – I would astound everyone by winning the Maths prize and, with a bit of luck, make some cash in hand.

After a little prompting from me, Robbo Robinson, one of the form's bright sparks, eventually put out a list of prices for Maths.

"You're 10-1 Church – fancy a bet?"

Robbo's voice sounded like bells at Christmas. But to plunge now would surely give the game away.

"Yeah, sure, I'll have two bob on that; in fact I would like to back two or three others. What prices are Jackie and Sheila?"

"Four to one apiece."

"OK, I'll have the same on them."

Expensive strategy, but prudent, I felt.

Two weeks later, Robinson did his rounds again. Three or four inches taller than any of his classmates, I saw him coming in more ways than one!

"How's your Maths book going?" I enquired.

"Steady, you know. No one's backing you though, so I've knocked you out to 100-8."

"Why that's an insult," I said gleefully. "Can I have another bet, say four shillings to win 50?"

"I suppose so," he said, "although how you think you can win beats me!"

Having all the answers didn't necessarily make me a certainty. In fact, working backwards entailed more commitment to homework than I had ever given before. Also, I had to be quite creative regarding which problems to get wrong, to avoid Long's suspicions.

The week before half-term, I chose to make my move and told every teacher who would listen, that I was going to spend my half-term break swotting-up my Maths. Once I got into the swing of it, it became an obsession, and for the second half of the term, I quickly reduced the incorrect answers to a minimum until I finally headed the class on my accumulative marks. In the end, I felt I more than deserved my narrow victory.

The teachers were delighted, particularly Mr Long, who ironically claimed some of the credit. Poor Robinson, however, never made a penny.

In some strange way, getting the 'answer book' turned out to be one of the few defining moments in my life, since although I could never again get a decent price about myself, the confidence I gained from this first academic success influenced and improved my school work beyond all recognition. In fact, in my final year, rather than allow me to monopolise the school prize-giving ceremonies (13 firsts from 14 subjects – unplaced in Physical Education – no swotting or answers required), the staff shrewdly passed a rule limiting each pupil to one subject award!

After the Summer holidays, having won a few pounds and the Maths prize the previous term, I believed I owed it to the school to put my entrepreneurial skills at their disposal. So, when the teachers began organising the Autumn Fair to raise funds for gym and sports equipment, my classmate Colin and I, with the backing of Bill Long and a supporting Art teacher Norman Brown, requested permission to run a Crown and Anchor game. The permission it seems, was only granted after a strong protest from Miss Snow (English), who saw it as the first step to a *'Rakes Progress'*. Snowy had, in the past, a track record of moral stands, particularly with her defence of the literal interpretation of Adam and Eve, which was always guaranteed to incense our Science Master. Grudgingly, however, she submitted to the persuasion of Bill and Norman, although she said she would be keeping a watchful eye on the game.

For the uninitiated, the game involves punters betting on the throw of three dice from a cup onto a cloth divided into six sections, these marked with a Heart, Diamond, Spade, Club, and a Crown and an Anchor. The same six symbols appeared on each dice; evens being paid out if the symbol bet on appeared once, 2-1 if twice and 3-1 if three times. Played in this, the usual way, the house should gain around eight per cent on turnover, but I was keen to give the punters a chance of a big win to keep them at the table longer.

After some thought, I introduced my personal innovation of dividing the centre of the board into six further sections – All Red,

All Black (note the Crown was red and the Anchor black), All Card Symbols and No Card Symbols. The two centre sections were to be Any Treble (this I laid at 33-1 and was to be my star attraction), and finally Any Double, the odds of which later led to some dispute. "Arty" Norman, who had produced a large, colourful replica of the board fixed on a post as our 'bookmaker's board,' had calculated that we should pay out Any Double at odds of 2-1.

The long awaited event took place in the main hall on a Wednesday afternoon and evening (most shops in Woking closed at 1pm on that day). By 3.30 pm, the hall was heaving with parents. They were entreated to cover a shilling with a penny in a bucket of water; to mark with a flag the hidden treasure (a pound note) buried under a table covered in grass, and to select the correct name of a doll from over 500 options. Watercolours, embroidery, breadboards and cakes, all made by the pupils were also on offer.

Betting on the Crown and Anchor board was slow at first, with some explanation of the various bets needed before the parents gained confidence. Mum and Dad had turned up in a supportive role and made gleeful noises when their small bets brought dividends, Mum in particular going OTT with her high pitched whoops. But on the arrival of Brian Fisher, a betting pal of mine (who later became a bookmaker) and his father, a local businessman, things began to hot up. Brian's dad knew a thing or three about betting, and after watching his son bet tuppence on this and thruppence on that, he started to back Any Double at 2-1. First taking the odds to a shilling and later betting four shillings to win eight on every throw of the dice. The shouts of delight from Brian and his dad each time a double came up brought over some of those queuing for refreshments, and trade now became brisk, with all the squares being backed. However, after the vigilant Ma Snow had got wind of some large payouts, the cashier ordered us to do a spot check on our funds. There was no doubt we were losing money. "Arty" Norman was called for, but would not concede that his calculations of 2-1 Any Double was the cause of our loses and pressed me to close the stall. But after my pleas and those of the punters, particularly Mr "give the boys a chance" Fisher, we were allowed 30 minutes to try to recoup our losses. I immediately crossed out, Any Double, and watched the Fishers melt away.

On the suggestion of my House Captain, I was given the school bell to peal and announce the names of any big winners. Within the 30 minutes, the deficit had been put right and crowds continued to gather, bets now being passed over the heads of those close to the board. Our best money spinner proved to be the elusive Any Treble at 33-1, and although it never came up, punters refused to leave the stall, optimistically hoping to recoup their loses on one last throw.

We continued to roll the dice until long after the last home-made cake was sold, the raffle announced and the doll was named Violet Elizabeth. And despite Ma Snow's comment, "That boy Church is doomed," Mr Peel, the Headmaster, came along especially to thank Colin and I for our "never say die spirit."

The following day in Assembly, the totals made by each stall were announced, and it was noted that the profit from the Crown and Anchor stall exceeded the sum of all the other stalls put together. A later discussion between the Maths Master and the Art teacher, ever after known as "Erroneous Norman," revealed that the true odds of Any Double were evens and not the disastrous 2-1 that nearly caused our ruin. Needless to say, I have never taken an artist's opinion on mathematics since!

The Revenge Coup

It is a betting truism that bookmakers want their punters to win occasionally, lest both their cash and interest run out. In this revelation, the continued losses of a gang of boys took an unexpected twist.

At Goldsworth Secondary Modern, there were always about a dozen boys who took an active interest in horseracing, varying from those who borrowed the racing page from their parents' *Daily Mirror*, to those who occasionally bought *The Sporting Life* or *Sporting Record*. To accommodate their interest, I unselfishly ran a book, not only on the big races but on the first two races at the principal meeting each day. Bets were singles or a double – win only. A few boys had a bet of twopence or threepence on most days, and although their losses were individually only a few pence a week, the profit supplemented my paper-round and kept my pet rabbits in the manner to which they had grown accustomed.

Most hardened punters come across a long losing run sometime in their life but, to those young children, guided by the Nation's experts and backed up with lucky rabbit's feet and wishbones, the possibility of going for three months without backing a winner seemed beyond belief.

The Derby of 1951 attracted the biggest field in living memory, 33 runners, so most of the two dozen or so bets I took on the race were well spread out. Ki Ming, however, owned by a Chinese restaurant owner, and winner of the 2,000 Guineas, had captured the boys' imagination, and as the 9-1 favourite was subject to a flood of bobs and tanners. But not one boy or girl had a penny on Arctic Prince, who romped in at 28-1. Two days later, Neasham Belle won the Oaks at 33-1, and again I swept the board. Things then went from bad to worse for some of the boys with money – Ki Ming was beaten again at Ascot, the French horse Pan won the Ascot Gold Cup at 100-8 and the boys' aversion to the French stopped them recouping their losses when the same horse added the Goodwood Cup.

By this time I was operating a debt collecting system of half-a-crown a week on the never-never and was probably the most unpopular boy in the school.

About three weeks later, with my daily take at a standstill, rumours of a revenge coup filtered through. Strangely, no bets were struck on Monday, Tuesday, Wednesday or Thursday but, on Friday both Dixie Dean and Brian Fisher wanted a five bob win double on Gordon Richards' mounts in the first two races at Windsor. It turned out they had told their tale of woe to old Jarvis, the paper-seller opposite Victoria Arch. Jarvis had seen better days when acting as a commission agent, putting on bets for some of the Epsom stables. Now in his late seventies, he was bent nearly double, and sported a permanent drip on the end of his nose! Still with a friend or two from the past, old Jarvis had told the boys to wait for Windsor, Gordon having certs in the first two races.

Talk of the revenge coup now became a reality, as about a dozen boys and two girls gave me pieces of paper torn from their exercise books wrapped around shilling pieces. All the bets read the same –

win double, Gordon Richards, first two races at Windsor. Most of the bets were given to me at the end of the lunch-break so there was no time to borrow a bike to cycle to Charlie Young's hairdressers to hedge it off.

Richards' first ride was Deuce, a smart two-year-old belonging to King George VI. His second mount, History, ran in a 2-y-o seller and, according to *Bouverie* of the *Daily Mirror*, was 'fully expected'.

In class that afternoon, while the pupils created a buzz of expectancy, the study of Pythagoras's Theorem and later the Beatitudes were for me, tinged with anxiety. At a quarter to four, tension mounting, we all tumbled out of school. Dixie Dean, speeding past me on his bike, shouted out "Say your prayers Churchy," as he shot off to buy a paper from old Jarvis.

Walking smartly along the Goldsworth Road without wanting to look hurried, I stopped at the sweet shop opposite the Goldsworth Arms. Mrs Noakes who ran the shop was reading the *Evening News*.

"Penny ice lolly – lime please – and have you got the Windsor results in the stop press?"

"No lime I'm afraid, only lemon."

"That's OK, but what about Windsor."

"What's going on, you're the third boy I've had in here asking the same question. Let me check again," she said, "*Windsor 2.00 ... Deuce 4-5 Fav.*, satisfied? ... you boys."

"What about the 2.30," I persisted.

"No, that's all it says. Sorry."

Coming out of the shop, I can remember thinking, "Well its bad, but not that bad."

A quarter of a mile walk to the news stand lay ahead. A hundred yards away, I could just make out the figure of old Jarvis sitting on the wall, crouched over. As I got closer, I could see a number of the children with bikes, waiting for me. Was this good or bad? I feared the worse. When they saw me coming a great cheer went up and old Jarvis beckoned me over.

"Come on Churchy, you've had a long run, pay up and look big – they've got you this time."

Feeling doomed, but straining to look nonchalant, I stammered "I'll t-t-t-take the *Standard* if the 2.30 result is there," avoiding the drip from his nose as I gave him my tuppence.

"Four-to-five and 8-11 lad, it won't break yer."

Encircled by my clientele, with eager faces and outstretched hands, I sadly played the unfamiliar role of Father Christmas.

Whist and White City

On the first Saturday after my 14th birthday, with the permission of Bernie Stevens, the MC and pillar of the local Catholic Church, I was allowed to play in the big-money Whist Drive at Woking's Railway Athletic Club.

In these pre-bingo days, upwards of 120 players would gather twice a week to play cards in the Athletic Club. But the atmosphere at these drives was far from athletic; the long hall accommodated over 30 card tables and was enveloped by a thick blue haze of cigarette smoke as the clicking of snooker balls and the clinking of beer glasses mingled with the chatter on horses, dogs and football. My Mother, Father and Nan attended these drives for many years, and occasionally, Nan would run small drives of six tables at home in the afternoons for her cronies.

One Tuesday night, two years earlier, Nan had gone to whist alone, and as she had not returned at the expected time, Mum and Dad began to get worried. Just as they were about to mount a search, there was a tap on the front door. In tottered Nan, her hat askew and clutching her stomach.

"I've got this pain," she said, staggering over to the kitchen table. "Just here."

Then, leaning over, she emptied her handbag across the table, releasing a shower of notes and silver. Worried frowns turned into whoops of delight as, sitting down and straightening her hat and fox fur, she told us how she had won the Snowball (a rollover jackpot) and had stayed behind to treat her friends to a good drink.

That Saturday, my fears of playing in the 'Big-time' were quickly dispelled, as many of Nan's friends came up to say hello and wish me luck. But when I sat down to play, I became so nervous that for the first hand or two, I had to press my hand of cards tight against the table to stop them from shaking.

For those outside Whist Drive circles, the game is played with temporary partners, who split up to go in different directions after each hand. The evening consists of 20 games (or hands), with prizes for the first three (most number of tricks), the top scores for each of the first and second halves, and also for the last six hands.

After the first half, there was a short break during which everyone crowded into the bar and stood around the snooker table. I added up my score – 62 – not great, but at least my hands had stopped shaking.

I started the second half quietly, but after a few hands recorded two consecutive tens. I then got a roasting from a formidable lady opponent for leading off with a 'Blowser' (a singleton – in order to trump the suit when led back to me). My blushes drew a comforting "Leave the boy alone Marjorie, he is doing his best" retort from my partner, which helped carry me through. A nine, eight and seven followed, but my quick calculation told me I needed a very good hand in the final game to have a squeak of landing the prize for the last six hands.

My partner for the last hand was Mr Barrymore, a jolly, red-faced man, who ran the paper stall on Woking Station, and it was for him that I delivered morning papers and did a spot of gardening after school. I could not have been in better company.

As the game progressed, it became clear that we both had short suits and, as the lead passed between us, we trumped and returned the play. Our ten tricks gave me a score of 54 for the last six hands – not a certainty but, after thanking Mr Barrymore for his sterling play, I waited with an assumed nonchalance that masked a thumping heart.

Bernie Stevens worked his way through the prizes until finally, he called for the last six. "Anyone with 57 – 56 – 55?" I craned my neck around to find no takers. "Fifty-four," he called scanning a sea of faces, then up shot my hand – "Young Michael, Dorothy's boy," he added. Moments later, to a smattering of applause, I went up to collect a gratifying 30-shilling prize.

That night, I thought I had taken the first step to a professional card-playing career, but sad to say, over the next two and a half years, I never won a major prize. And although I enjoyed the gossip and the company of betting zealots, it was apparent that my card-playing skills were someway behind my talents for the laying and taking of odds.

There were many colourful characters at Whist that night, a few of whom regularly went greyhound racing with Dad and me at Wimbledon and White City. Don and Vicky always added a tinge of scandal, both divorced and living in digs together (very risqué in 1950). Don was an ex-Guardsman, with slicked back hair and a pencil slim moustache. Vicky was tiny and bubbly, full of fun and covered in jewellery. Some said they were like a pair of old movie stars. Then there was the Giant, a seven foot man who could fan out all 52 cards in his hands. In his younger days he had boxed in fairgrounds and had acted as a double in some early fight films. Sadly he was very ugly and Stan always upset Mum by addressing him as Boris (after Boris Karloff). Add to these Ginger, a part-time builder. His connections numbered two or three greyhound trainers and a string of kennel girls, but the information he received rarely seemed to have any favourable effect on his finances.

On one special occassion two years later, the six of us went to White City for the final of the Greyhound Derby. Meeting up in the tea-bar on the station, we all had our fancies. Endless Gossip was inevitably the choice of Don and Vicky, as they had been the subject of it for years and now hoped to profit by it. Dad and I had to agree, for he was supposedly the fastest greyhound around. Ginger however, was all for Dashboard Dan; his grapevine had told him that the dog had 'eaten up well' after his surprising semi-final victory over Endless Gossip and he was now a steal at 7-1. The Giant, or Boris, thought the other semi-final winner, Drumman Rambler would go close from an inside draw. While the chatter was in full flow, the train pulled in and we all clambered aboard.

At Weybridge, Spooner got in, a short fat man in a greasy raincoat. He had acquired his name from the misfortune of being completely bald apart from a clump of hair on one side of his head that he spooned over in a cover-up attempt that fooled nobody. In spite of his follicle deficiency, he was a very jolly fellow who talked endlessly. His method, if you could call it that, continually tempted fate, for he would bet all his money on the first two races, playing it up if successful. Once or twice a year he would win enough money to buy a good greyhound, but almost always he had a tale of woe, such as he had picked the last four winners without a cent to go on them. In those days, dog tracks were full of characters like Spooner, who would be in the thick of it for a few years and then disappear completely.

Unlike any other night in Greyhound racing, people travelled to the Derby at White City from all over Britain and Ireland. Track regulars from Belle Vue and Brighton would turn up in trainloads if they had a runner in the final, while fans from Clapton and Wembley, who nearly always had a finalist, would cheer like a football crowd when their runner was announced in the Derby parade.

This was the golden age of greyhound racing. The culture and the scenes that follow will never return but, for this teenager, like my early Derby trips to Epsom, they ingrained in me both a way of life and a sense of history never to be forgotten.

As our party tumbled out of White City Station, both sides of the road were packed with people heading for the track, some spilling over into the jammed traffic. Street vendors yelled the familiar "Roasted peanuts, tanner a bag," while all along the road buskers and beggars attended their regular pitches. One I remember was an ex-boxer sitting on the pavement, detached from his wooden legs, with a placard around his neck and a tin cup for coins in front of him. The Giant always made a point of crossing the road to say hello to him, and drop him half-a-crown.

Once inside the track, we wished each other luck and went our separate ways. Stan and I headed for the seafood bar for a plate of jellied eels and crusty bread. On visiting the nearest toilets, we found a Crown and Anchor dice game in progress at the entrance, while the 'Three card trick' merchants were in play at the exit. Lookouts, of course, were posted at both ends.

Race followed race until the long interval came before the Derby, a breathing space to ease the concentration. By tradition, the massed bands of the Royal Marines took centre stage, striking up with their regimental march, *A Life on the Ocean Wave* and treating the 40,000 crowd to an immaculate marching display. Throughout the night, queues at the Tote windows reached alarming lengths. In fact, most punters queuing to collect their winnings usually had to miss the following race.

At the bottom end of the track there was an enormous white board with six clock faces, one for each trap, the arrow on each pointing to the return to a two-shilling win stake. Endless Gossip was clear favourite and, as the money poured on, so the arrow on trap six swung to four shillings (even money). While the band was playing, many punters hurried down to the paddock to get a pre-race inspection of the finalists. And whilst the dogs were having their jackets fitted, a young Irish lad straddled the paddock wall and began playing *'Phil the Fluter's Ball'* on a harmonica – which caused great amusement among a party of Chinese who waved their hats at him in approval.

As the Marines trooped off, so the Derby parade began, and as the dogs were walked slowly around the track, people came down from the crowded terraces to form a final opinion. Following the parade at a respectable distance was a man in a white boiler suit and peaked-cap, carrying a dustpan and brush to sweep up the inevitable droppings. On any other night he would go unnoticed, but tonight he often raised a cheer as he went about his business.

Standing on tip-toe, I could just see the last pair of greyhounds being put into the traps. The buzz of the crowd now fell to a murmur, until the starter, attired in a bowler hat and full riding gear, waved his flag to the hare-driver. As the hare began to move, so the noise increased with a gathering momentum that reached a crescendo as the greyhounds sprung from the traps. The Derby roar was in full throttle. Endless Gossip (6) was not too well away but, showing terrific speed in the run-up, he caught and passed Drumman Rambler (2) and Shaggy Newshound (1) between the first two bends. As he went further ahead down the back straight, the noise was deafening. Seconds later the official result, traps 6-2-1 went up on the board, followed shortly by the time, 28.50 seconds, a new track record.

Before Dad and I collected our winnings, we pushed through to the rails for a closer look at the winner during his lap of honour. It was here Stan and I bumped into Don and Vicky, flushed with excitement and money.

"I thought I would take Vicky to a night club to celebrate," said Don. "Perhaps we'll stay overnight," he added giving me a wink. In contrast, Endless Gossip had only provided me with the fare home. Even so, nothing could take away from the colour and excitement of that magical Greyhound Derby night.

According to history, Endless Gossip, the son of Priceless Border and Narrogar Ann, both Derby winners, went on to win the Laurels at Wimbledon, also in record time, and later won a show prize at Crufts. Experts rated him the best English-bred, track greyhound of all time.

Ace Information

Dad's brothers, Albert and Henry were always short of money: Albert due to his unsuccessful betting and Henry because the pittance he earned from his gardening job barely covered the rent that Albert charged him for his dilapidated terraced house. Despite this imbalance, they remained good friends. So much so, that one day, sitting up at Henry's kitchen table (tea and Woodbines to hand), Albert, reading the adverts in the sporting press, came up with the idea that they could both earn a bit of spare cash by advertising 'confidential racing information.'

At first Henry thought this a little ironic, since his brother's financial predicament was entirely due to his tenuous understanding of the sport. However, as Albert revealed the details of his scam and the very little capital needed to start-up, Henry, ever susceptible to Albert's influence, warmed to the idea.

"First we put an advert in one of the racing papers – Ace Information sounds the business – then, ask the readers to send us a five shilling postal order for three Saturday advices."

"Where do we get the information from?" quizzed Henry.

"Easy," said Albert, eyes twinkling, "we buy the *Sporting Record* midweek, pick out three of their tips for the weekend and, as soon as the postal orders come rolling in, we'll send them our special advices – no sweat – no risk – money for old rope."

"We've still got to put together the advert and write the letters," worried Henry, aware of his own limitations.

At this stage, Albert hadn't given much thought to the details but, on hearing me chatting to Aunty Mary in the scullery, called out, "You made the frame in English this term, didn't you Michael?"

"Well, yes, if you count finishing fourth," I replied cautiously.

"Well then, you can be our secretary," Albert enthused. And with that, I joined them to work out the details, requesting the expenses necessary to cover the advert, stationery and stamps. It seemed the 'advices' would be hand written until the brothers became famous and bought a typewriter.

After two weeks, we had received only three postal orders and given no winners. But the third week Albert tipped Cherry Herring, a 9-1 winner at Lingfield, and promptly advertised his success in the next edition of the paper. The response was instant – 14 postal orders. And the week after, when Assouan (100-30), and Cadet Roussel (20-1), both won on St Leger day, I had to take a day off from school (suffering conveniently from hayfever and asthma), to get more than 30 letters off in time. That evening, I put it to Albert that my increased workload was worth ten bob a week and, wincing slightly, he shook my hand on it.

Later that month, maintaining a handsome level stakes profit, Albert tipped Eastern Emperor, another big priced winner. But it was not until I was compiling an advert listing our winners to date that it suddenly hit me. All our tips began with the letters A, C or E ....ACE.

"So that's why Albert had insisted our service be called Ace Information," I thought. When I quizzed him on it he became defensive.

"Would you rather I tipped a string of losers then Michael?" he protested.

I backed off.

Henry, now with the dry rot repaired in his upstairs bedrooms and a new dart board, said nothing. And although my heart sank at the naivety of it all, Albert's belief in his tipping abilities soared, and the next time I met him he positively glowed.

"I've been checking through my tipping record since we started and I've decided that we should reinvest our profits in our own tips!"

"But what if we lose?" queried Henry, now used to moving freely about in his upstairs bedrooms.

"Lose?" retorted Albert defiantly, "we'll worry about that when it happens."

"I think I'll hang on to my ten shillings a week if that's alright with you, Uncle," I said.

That weekend and the next, Albert and Henry's reinvestment paid off. Albert was now talking seriously about buying a new fish van, while Henry was tentatively considering a new spade.

Albert now took his dreams a stage further.

"Look Henry, why are we waiting until Saturday to bet, when I can pick three specials every day?"

"But the *Sporting Record* doesn't come out until Wednesday," said Henry, as usual not up to Albert's speed.

"Oh sod the *Sporting Record*," Albert snorted, "I'll pick my own winners." And he did – all beginning with the letters A, C and E.

Albert was now a regular at Charlie Young's betting room. Alice said he should bring his bed with him, since he was also applying his 'winning system' to the greyhounds at Wimbledon and White City.

The increased size of our tipping adverts, although bringing in more business, coincided with a run of short priced winners for Albert. And now, having advised his clientele to bet in pounds rather that shillings, he was convinced that it was their money bringing the prices down. Beset by a combination of paranoia and megalomania, he stopped advertising, leaving Henry to his faithful garden and me, out of a part-time job.

Albert now entered a crisis. Continually faced with more than one choice of the magic capital letters in a race, he invariably picked the wrong one, and in desperation he decided to back them all. Tragically, this occurred simultaneously with a complete absence of these letters from the results page. A week later he was broke.

The following month, while I was playing darts with Henry in his back yard, Albert's round, beaming face appeared over the gate.

"I've got some good news chaps – I know where we went wrong."

We cautiously put down the darts to listen.

"T – O – P," he explained, "Top Information."

Todman (8-1), Oscar (7-1), Pinkthorn (10-1),

How about it lads?"

A Tip from Charlie Smirke

For many years, Charlie Young had been the most popular hairdresser in Woking and his backroom gambling set-up handled more than a third of the town's betting turnover. Charlie's acquaintances were legendary and, a few days before the 1952 Derby, one such character – Solly Bernhart – was an unexpected visitor to his Salon.

"Something for the weekend Solly?" Charlie enquired.

"No thanks," replied Solly, whose sexual experiences where now purely academic. "Actually, I've come down to-day to do you a little favour."

"Let's go through to the back room then," said Charlie, remembering some of Solly's previous favours.

Solly Bernhart was a flamboyant character, who resembled Mr Pickwick in appearance but not in motivation. He had been a friend of Charlie's since before the war, and having recently sold his jeweller's shop in the East-end, was now flirting with a life of leisure.

Once in the betting room, Charlie introduced Solly to Alice and I, who were pouring over the day's runners.

"You've met my wife Alice, and this is young Michael, runs a penny book at Goldsworth School, but comes in to hedge-off the occasional hefty double."

Solly shook hands, but hastily declined Alice's offer of tea and Woodbines in favour of Charlie's Cognac.

I was all ears as Solly told his tale of how, on a recent visit to the Savoy Turkish baths in Jermyn Street, he had bumped into Charlie Smirke.

"He was full of himself," said Solly, "whistling away, he was, told me Tulyar was the best Derby mount he could remember. In fact he kept on saying 'I'll Tulyar this and I'll Tulyar that,' to hammer home the message."

Young rubbed his chin thoughtfully.

"Have you backed it yet Solly," he enquired.

"Well, I had £30 at 100-6 with my local man, but that's his limit, and I'd like to get a bit more on with you."

"That's OK," said Charlie, sipping his cognac, "I'll make some calls, take a price and you can pay me cash, how much are we looking at?"

"Fifty or sixty quid if you can – we can't miss this one," responded Solly. Charlie made the calls on the 'business phone,' keeping his voice to a whisper. Suddenly he looked up "100-7 do yer, Solly?"

"Fine."

"He will lay you a £1,000 to £70," said Charlie, "but," covering the mouthpiece, "I'll want the cash here before the race, say Monday."

"Of course, of course," Solly nodded vigorously, "don't forget yourself."

Charlie lowered his voice and completed the added investment.

Sinking their second Cognac, they congratulated themselves on their expected good fortune. Feeling rejected at being left out of the negotiations, I got up to go.

"Off now," said Alice, then, "here Charlie, aren't you going to cut Michael in for something?"

"Yes of course, I almost forgot about the boy. What would you like Michael?"

"Well, as I am actually going to Epsom; perhaps you'll give me the price to five shillings?"

"Yes that's OK," Charlie replied nonchalantly. "You have a few bob to come, so I'll take it out of that."

"You're all heart Charlie," I replied and promptly legged it back to school.

Monday came and went with no sign of Solly. Tuesday lunch-time, he still hadn't shown. Charlie began to panic. Alice suggested that he try to cancel the bet, but his reputation was at stake and Charlie wouldn't hear of it. However, after failing to trace Solly, he phoned his big players to try to lay off – they were not interested. Charlie's panic mounted and he suffered a troubled night.

Early Wednesday morning, having got special permission from Headmaster, Bonk Peel, to have Derby Day off, I dropped into the hairdressers to hand in my family's bets. Charlie and Alice, looking the worst for wear, were already occupied with a steady stream of shilling each-way's and any-to-come's. Alice confided, "Charlie's furious with Solly – it isn't the first time you know. If he doesn't show and Tulyar loses, we're buggered – its like doing a thousand hair cuts for nothing."

Charlie came over, "Don't listen to her, she's got no bottle," he said bravely.

"But you could do me a favour as you're going to Epsom."

"Sure," I piped up, eager to help.

"Look, phone here as near as you can to the big race, if Solly hasn't brought the dosh, I want you to spread £30 over the first three in the Derby betting – the race is wide open and I know you'll beat the S.P. Hopefully it will save our bacon."

I stashed the small fortune carefully into my blazer pocket. I'm going to be the biggest punter on our coach I thought, and it could be the start of the big time for me.

Arriving at Epsom with my bottle of Tizer, telescope, sandwiches and raincoat, my heart sank on seeing the length of the telephone queues. If I was going to phone, it had to be now – still no Solly.

Walking across the course I was surprised that Tulyar was not only as low as 10-1, but now third favourite. I waited. The showers forecast for the afternoon didn't arrive. Instead, the sun beat down on the packed crowd, causing hats and coats to be relegated to carrier bags.

Just before the Derby, the money for Tulyar became an avalanche, forcing him into favouritism. Some bookmakers, in danger of a one-horse-book, off loaded their commitments onto other bookmakers, so forcing the price down further to 11-2. In consequence, the five French-trained horses who had previously vied for favouritism, were all on the drift. I was now faced with the problem of which three of the five Frenchies to back for Charlie, as they were forever interchanging and increasing in price. And it now became obvious from the crowds pressing in on the bookies, that I had to choose between seeing the race or trying to beat the S.P. My 16-year-old priorities won the day – I watched the race.

Throughout the Derby parade, the heat, and the endless inane chatter of two uncommitted ladies immediately in front of me, caused me to feel queasy. I must have slumped forward as, moments later, I felt myself being passed over heads to a perfect position, normally reserved for members of the constabulary. I sustained a miracle cure.

My first view of the race was when the field turned into the straight – 33 runners were an eyeful, but I could pick out Tulyar,

moving up on the outside. Steadying my telescope, I got a better view two-furlongs out as Charlie Smirke gave him a crack and they stormed into the lead, the green and brown hoops of the Aga Khan getting bigger and bigger until my hopes became reality. Apparently, at the finish, my unrestrained celebrations had convinced a nearby policemen that I had made a full recovery and I was promptly escorted back into the enclosure.

Later, checking the number board with my racecard, I noted that the second, Gay Time, had been ridden by the young Lester Piggott, and Faubourg, one of the French horses had finished third. The relief of Tulyar's victory and the saving of Charlie Young's £30, together with my skin, seemed to have solved everything. So after a near-perfect day, and after being dropped off in Woking, I hurried to the hairdressers.

"Come in Michael," Charlie said beaming from ear to ear.

"Did Solly turn up?" I blurted out.

"No, and not a word on the phone. Just as well, thank God, what a result. Do you know, I've won about £1,200."

"I think it is a little more than that," I said.

"How do you mean?" he puzzled.

"I saved the £30 for you."

Alice intervened with a certain lack of perception, "Blimey Charlie, how's that for honesty? I think he deserves a reward."

"Ummm," said Charlie, obviously considering the pros and cons of my actions.

"Tell you what, Michael, I'll double your winnings and we can all celebrate."

Later, clutching my seven quid and change, I made my way home with ambivalent feelings – the glow of nobility from my honest gesture vying with my mental calculation of just how many paper-rounds at six shillings a week equalled £30. On hearing my story,

Mum had no such ambivalence in reaching her conclusion.

"Charlie Young is a mean bastard!"

Post Mortem:

Solly Bernhart died of a heart attack on Monday, May 26, 1952, two days before the Derby.

Tulyar went on to win the Eclipse Stakes, King George VI and Queen Elizabeth Stakes, and the St Leger Stakes. He was unbeaten as a 3-y-o.

Alice and Charlie had their first holiday since the war, staying at the Carlton Hotel in Cannes.

A Coronation Party and Pinza's Derby

Tuesday, June 2, 1953, was the day of the Queen's Coronation. Hundreds of thousands of people came from all over the world to line the route and, thousands more had purchased their first television set specifically for this occasion. Our next-door neighbours, Mr and Mrs Powell, had taken the plunge, and were the first in our avenue to do so.

Generously, they invited a dozen or more friends to watch the event. It seemed to last all day, and although they provided a bottle of sherry and a tin of custard cream biscuits, we were encouraged to bring our own sandwiches and flasks of tea, together with a kitchen chair or two. Packed into a small room, with the curtains drawn (so as to provide a clearer picture), the ten inch screen in a large wooden cabinet was our focal-point for the day.

Children sat on the floor in the front; ladies on kitchen chairs, with the men managing as best they could on a plank arrangement at the back. The Powell's furniture had been moved into their second bedroom the night before.

Both the communal spirit and the refreshments held out pretty well until my Nan, a Royal Family devotee from way back, had her enjoyment of the proceedings diminished somewhat by Cousin Peter tipping a full glass of Tizer into her best handbag. The ensuing commotion diverted the attention of those present for a full ten minutes.

Soon after the actual crowning of the Queen, an odd assortment of glasses containing sherry were passed around, and upon Mr Powell's toast, we all stood up, solemnly clinked glasses, and said "God Bless Queen Elizabeth."

Some of the older generation reminisced about previous coronations and old Mr Hopkirk (who lived two doors away), had brought photographs showing him as a Queen's footman in full livery, standing on the back of Queen Victoria's coach for a ceremonial procession.

To round off the day, in what proved to be a novel finale, a 'pass the parcel' game was played. Actually it turned out to be a hybrid, owing something to musical chairs, and it took some time to get going, as the rules had to be explained several times to Uncle Arthur and old Mr Hopkirk, who were both hard of hearing. Throughout these preparations, Auntie Mary took care to keep Peter a safe distance from any remaining beverages.

Once in progress, the game seemed to go quite well. Mr Powell controlled the music while a mountain of red, white and blue wrapping paper grew in the centre. At long last, the contest was reduced to the final two contestants – Mr Powell's young son Bobby and old Mr Hopkirk. Mr Powell then turned his back on the proceedings in an effort to be impartial, leaving the radio playing longer than before. When he finally switched it off, the cheers from the onlookers turned to laughter, as both contestants continued to pass the parcel back and forth. Mr Hopkirk, because he hadn't realised the music had stopped, and Bobby, because he hadn't quite grasped the rules.

At this point Mr Powell, choosing to be diplomatic rather than impartial, grabbed the parcel and presented it to Mr Hopkirk, while discretely providing a half-crown to placate his son. Mr Hopkirk, having grown tired of a game that baffled him, decided to light his pipe, but slumping forward, he accidentally dropped the lighted match into the mass of wrapping paper. Within seconds, the floor was alight – people scattered everywhere, eager to undertake helpful tasks. Peter seized his opportunity and was seen heading towards the flames with a large jug of orange squash, but Mr Powell, being a fireman, kept an extinguisher in the kitchen and quickly doused the flames. No doubt this was one fire he did not discuss back at the Fire Station.

The day's excitement at an end, Mr Powell now made the slightly bizarre presentation of a bone-china Coronation Mug to old Mr Hopkirk, thanking him sincerely for his contribution to the event.

* * *

The Saturday after the Coronation was Derby Day. The newly knighted Sir Gordon Richards, had yet to win the race in 27 attempts. This year, in what turned out to be his final attempt, his mount was Sir Victor Sassoon's Pinza, a big, strong bay that looked destined to start favourite. Charlie Young, our hairdresser-cum-bookmaker, was adamant after Tudor Minstrel's defeat that there was a jinx on Richards in the Derby and as a result of his conviction, he laid me 10-1 (double the starting price) to a ten bob note.

Travelling alone, I boarded the first Derby Day bus to leave Woking for Epsom. I carried my day's requirements in mum's shopping bag: cheese and pickle sandwiches, ginger beer, a plastic telescope, the *Daily Mirror* and a little notebook in which I had painted all the colours of the Derby runners, to help me remember them for the parade – although I needed no reminding of Pinza's peacock and gold hoops.

Throughout the coach journey punters talked of their fancies for the big race – the ladies plumping as one for the young Queen's horse,

Aureole, while many of the men were persuaded by *The Sporting Life's* headlines, tipping Premonition.

On arrival and before taking up my favoured position in the back corner of the old Stewards' Stand alongside the winning post, I visited the nearest gents' toilet on the downs. This took the form of a long tent guarded by an old man shouting out loudly, "ACCOMMODATION," and charging tuppence to enter. The inside had to be seen to be believed – two long trenches, three foot deep and three foot wide, had been thoughtfully dug for our convenience. Gentlemen were invited to stand either side, facing each other, and even at this early hour the trenches were filling up alarmingly. Hastily retreating from the pungent air of this facility, I wondered how the ladies were accommodated in their tent a little distance away.

Renewing my enthusiasm for the day, I came across a circle of racegoers and instantly recognised Prince Monolulu standing on a box in the centre, bedecked in a plumed headdress and sundry rabbits' feet. His cry of 'I gotta horse,' was a regular part of the Derby scene, and this year, he assured us, that if Sir Gordon won the Derby, the Queen would make him Lord Gordon. As I continued across the Downs, crowds gathered to see an escapologist bound in chains and wrapped in a shroud, while further attractions promised fire-eaters, sword swallowers, a lamb with two heads and countless seedy strip-shows.

By 3-30, the crowd had grown into an enormous gathering; some said more than half a million people, many staying over from the Coronation. Looking through my telescope from my special vantage point, I could see Arabs, Greeks and Turks, all in National dress, and the traditional smattering of Pearly Kings and Queens.

As the Derby parade started, my homework on the jockeys' silks helped me identify all the runners, but as the tension grew and the sun beat down on the back of my head, I felt I was going to faint.

Instead, with a certain presence of mind, I leaned over the back wall of the stand and was promptly sick over the bonnet of a Rolls Royce below. However, my embarrassment, the sympathy of those nearby, and the angry shouts of the chauffeur below, failed to hinder my determination to focus my telescope on the start.

The great shout of 'They're Off' suddenly gave me the feeling of being at the centre of the world as the line of colours threaded its way to the top of the hill. Here I picked out the Aga Khan's Shikampur and, before long, was urged by those around me to give them a running commentary. This I did enthusiastically, for there was no racecourse commentary, as there is today.

Into the straight, and I could see Pinza gaining on Shikampur, with Aureole moving up. Suddenly, a great roar went up as Gordon Richards went to the front about a furlong out. Harry Carr did try to challenge on Aureole, but by now the peacock and gold hoops of Pinza had flown to victory, amid scenes of great jubilation.

Everyone was delighted for Gordon, whether they had backed him or not. A few minutes later, an elderly couple nearby gave me a cup of tea and two Aspros, hoping that I now felt better. They had travelled overnight from Scotland and said it had been worth every penny. They also suggested I could possibly be the next Raymond Glendenning, if I could only settle my tummy on the big occasions.

Hours later, as the coach crawled away from the Downs, we were given the time-honoured serenade from the gypsy children, banging on the coach and shouting "Throw out yer mingy's," (a plea for loose change). Soon we were speeding home, and I settled down to relive the events of a memorable day with great satisfaction.

Grease, Greyhounds and Crimewatch

"Scrape those meat tins out before you go Church. I want to see them gleaming before you put one foot outside this camp." Sergeant Thompson's voice boomed across the 'tin room' at the back of the canteen.

Thompson, the catering sergeant at RAF West Kirby, had promised the Commanding Officer that he would win the all-England award for the best and cleanest RAF canteen. And here was I, five weeks into my National Service, released from square bashing and band practice (3rd cornet) to assist in bulling up the canteen. To make matters worse, this evening was my first off-camp pass, with which I had planned to visit Seaforth Stadium, one of the three local greyhound tracks.

Two hours later, with the help of half a dozen Brillo pads, I presented eight large meat tins for inspection.

"Call those clean Church? They look bloody mankey and smell bloody mankey. Get them into boiling water and this time use wire wool."

It took a further hour's drudgery before I was released but, with great determination, I caught the bus and train to get to Seaforth for the last three races.

To my surprise, all the races were four-dog handicaps, the traps placed at intervals; trap four at the front on the outside and trap one at the back on the rails, with an inside hare. Punters had to have a degree in maths to work out the comparative times, but the finishes were usually close and the forecast was the most popular bet. After two failed attempts at the forecast, I decided to back trap four to win the last race.

Joining the back of a queue, I eventually got to the tote window just as the dogs were being put into the traps and, having a slight stammer, my attempts to spit out "One win four," became "Wer-wer-one." Before I could finish, a ticket whirred out, my pound was taken, the lights went out and the sellers hatch slammed down. Surprised, I banged on the hatch, shouting "What about my change?" Now, with the dogs already racing, I checked my ticket under one of the down lights on the terrace. It read £1 WIN TRAP ONE. One pound! I only wanted two shillings, and that was on the four dog.

Looking across at the greyhounds, four led the other three into the last bend. But then, running wide, he let in the one dog, who powered up the straight to win by a length. Still in shock, I waited for the official result and tote dividends.

"Win number one, seven pounds ten shillings."

The rest I never heard – seven pounds ten; three weeks' wages! I dashed over to the payout and could now clearly see the £1 sign over the window. Handing over my ticket with a trembling hand, the young lady said "Feeling better now – you were getting in a right state." Just behind me I heard an old man mutter, "Where do these young Airman get their money?" I would have liked to have told him but it might have taken me all night to spit it out.

The following week I went to Liverpool's White City, a narrow track with the spectators under cover all the way round and standing on floor boarding. It looked then as if it had seen better days and only had six bookmakers. Once again the races were four-dog handicaps, but tonight there were two inter-track races with another Liverpool dog track, Stanley.

I suppose there was acute rivalry between these tracks, but I wasn't aware of this, at least until the second of the heats. In the first, the White City favourite won, but their other dog finished last, so, because points were allotted on a four-three-two-one basis, the tracks were tied at five all. In the second heat, a Stanley dog was favourite – a fast starting brindled bitch in trap four.

Standing near the fourth bend, the race already in progress, and with the four dog six lengths clear, I noticed a tall, swarthy man nearby remove his large cape-like raincoat, and, just as the dogs turned into the home straight, he threw it over the leading bitch. A pile-up resulted with the last two dogs convinced the hare was also under the coat. The man then ran off, pursued by two officials, one of whom caught and held him fast until a policemen arrived.

It seemed the villain had claimed mistaken identity, but one of his pursuers called on the policeman to "get the young airman over to identify him." This I was duly pressurised into, and signed a short statement, before the culprit was handcuffed to another policeman and taken away. The race was declared void, and soon after the punters settled down to studying the next.

Leaving the track half-an-hour later, I spotted two shady-looking men in a doorway opposite.

"That's him, the airman," I heard one of them say. I took off.

After running 40 yards or so, I joined a bus queue and removed my peaked-cap. My heart was still pounding when they caught up with me before the bus arrived.

"We're from the *Liverpool Echo*, would you give us the story?"

I never returned to White City, but instead visited the Stanley track twice during my last week at West Kirby. Meanwhile, Sergeant Thompson's dream came true as the camp's canteen won the all-England award. Photographs of its modern furniture with latticed dividers, highly polished floors and flowers on every table, appeared in the *Echo* alongside *'Airman Identifies Culprit in Greyhound Scandal!'*

Part of the excitement of going greyhound racing whilst in the RAF was the freedom of mixing with civilians – ordinary people, who would gladly chat to you about the dogs. This, compared with the strictly, ordered routine of the camp, seemed to me like heaven. On both my trips to Stanley I transferred over to the 'posh side.' On one occasion, standing alone by the winning post, I was asked by a lady in a fur coat who I was going to back in the next.

"Roller Coaster," I replied.

"Oh that's ours," she said. "Trevor and I own it."

Just then, Trevor appeared in a bright camel coat, nodded on our introduction, and then buried his head in the *Greyhound Express*. I drifted away and so did Roller Coaster, finishing third of four.

Later that week I saw Trevor and Sadie again. This time, they had been drinking and he raised his hat.

"Trevor's on a roll," Sadie said, "He's backed the last three winners."

"Quiet dear, let's hear what the Royal Air Force fancy for the next."

"Well, I think the scratch dog's got too much to do and both three and four will fade, so its got to be two."

"Trap two – Young Hazard," he laughed, "Young Hazard it is then. I'll cut you in for a pound."

We watched the race together, the blue jacket the focus of our attention under the bright lights. Three led four into the straight, but two finished like a train, with the three of us jumping up and down and shouting him home.

After the last race I was invited to meet their friends in the owners' bar, a rare treat for me, especially as all of them wanted to buy me a drink. "This is more like it," I thought, putting the meat-tin episode behind me and downing my fifth gin and tonic.

All too soon, Trevor and Sadie were driving me back to camp in their new Jaguar, and the inevitable sight of the barbed wire fences and rows of wooden huts brought me back to earth. Pulling in at the main gate we were approached by a Military Police Sergeant. Trevor wound down his window.

"Oh it's you sir! Sorry, didn't recognise the new car – oh and thank you for the case of whisky for the canteen celebrations."

"I hope you were able to enjoy a drop," Trevor said graciously.

"Is that one of our Airmen with you sir?" the Sergeant enquired.

"Yes."

"Has he been in any trouble sir?"

"No, on the contrary ...."

The Sergeant peered into the car.

"It's you Church, I see .... been on another one of your crusades against crime have you?"

Moments later he eyed me with suspicion, as, with assumed dignity, I attempted to walk in a straight line through the main gate.

Later, safely in my narrow bed, I dreamt of myself gracing the owners' bar once more, this time, as the proud owner of a string of successful greyhounds.

Miss Deecie to the Rescue

When I arrived as a new posting at RAF Hospital Ely, early in November 1954, nobody knew my name, but the day after, it was on the lips of every airman and woman.

Escorted to my hut and shown my bed by the overseeing corporal, I was told of the big parade the following day. After a sharp overnight frost, we lined up on the parade ground in front of the visiting Group Captain. I was positioned in the front line of the second row and, upon the order to 'Present Arms', slipped, falling backwards onto my head, but still clutching my rifle. To my astonishment, before I could get to my feet, two stretcher-bearers appeared from nowhere to carry me off, not just to the sidelines, but to the sickbay. After my name, rank and number were taken, I was swiftly x-rayed, admitted to Ward 10 and a report given to the Group Captain before his departure.

All was made clear by the Matron the following morning. On the same parade the previous year, an airman had also slipped coming to attention, and after several hours of concussion, he was eventually sent to a neurological hospital in London. The resident Wing Commander had therefore put into place precautions in case of a recurrence

Actually, I had never felt better but, because I spoke with a slight stammer, I was kept in for observation for a further eight days. As I settled into my 'inpatient holiday' and was supplied with newspapers, fruit and a radio, I became deeply grateful. Best of all, I was given the luxury of hours and hours to study the results in my Form Book and it was here that I first discovered Miss Deecie. But more of her later.

News spread fast; the *Ely Standard*, the Catholic Parish Priest and the Entertainment's Officer visited me in turn, the last named conspiring with the priest to persuade me to play *'The Last Post'* in church on Armistice Sunday. For this favour, I was promised 40 cigarettes. Trapped, I agreed, even though I didn't smoke and wasn't a Catholic.

By springtime, I had settled into my job as Orthopaedic Clerk, sharing my office with Ben Jordan, Medical Clerk/Pianist, and Pete Mitchell, Senior Ward Orderly/Double Bass. For gigs and service concert parties we were joined by Bobby Barnes, Postroom/Drums and an assortment of WAAFs and Airmen who either sang or took part in sketches. All went under the auspices of Tom Lewis, Station Warrant Officer/Entertainment's Officer, and Tom, as it happened, also took a keen interest in the affairs of the Turf.

Stationed in Cambridgeshire and within striking distance of Newmarket, many of the Airman and WAAFs followed racing. The post room doubled as our headquarters of racing intelligence, with Bobby keeping in touch with the local bookmaker as his prime duty.

This particular year, there was a National newspaper strike from March 25 (Grand National Day) to April 30. Throughout this period, Bobby supplied us with stencilled lists of runners to keep us up-to-date, the results being broadcast on the radio every evening.

This was the age of betting systems and it seemed every racing man had one. When there were no newspapers, it was Doug Smith's mounts in cross-doubles or favourites in each way trebles; when there were papers it was the most selected in *The Sporting Life* or

Newsboy's nap. But after two months of Flat Racing, all the regular systems were showing a loss and their followers were looking for something new.

It was then I remembered Miss Deecie, the tipster from Epsom that I had read about in hospital: "Established 25 years – three one-horse letters for £1." Putting things into perspective, I was being paid about £2 a week, so four of us shared the cost by paying five shillings each. To our surprise, the three letters arrived in rapid succession and were all for horses running at Epsom on Friday, May 27: Meld in the Oaks, Narrator in the Coronation Cup and Penthouse in the Royal Stakes. After a quick conference, Ben, Pete, Bobby and I decided to combine our cash and back them in three £1 win doubles and a £1 win treble.

Oaks day duly arrived and, being a Friday, there were full Medical and Orthopaedic clinics to attend. Ben borrowed a portable radio, which we secreted under a tea-cosy on my desk to hear the commentary on the Oaks and Coronation Cup. By 3pm, the clinics were in full swing, with patients forming a docile queue down the corridor.

"We now take you over to Raymond Glendenning at Epsom, for a commentary on the 157th running of the Oaks."

"Turn it up, turn it up," cried Ben, returning from the Women's Institute trolley with a freshly made pot of tea and chocolate cup cakes.

The increase in volume, however, was quickly reversed as the Medical Wing Commander appeared to enquire how many more patients he had.

"I say, is that the big race?" he said, eyeing the tea-cosy with a puzzled expression.

"Yes sir."

"You lads keen on racing?"

"Yes sir."

"Hmm, I've had two bob each way on Belladonna 33-1 you know."

"Yes sir, good luck sir."

"Let me know the result will you?"

"Yes sir."

Ten minutes later, Ben took down the next batch of medical records. On the top was a new record card; it read *1st Meld 7-4, 2nd Ark Royal, 3rd Reel In.*

Four o'clock, and tension mounted in the Appointments room. From under the tea-cosy we heard: "They're coming into line and they're off for the Coronation Cup."

"Pop outside and tell Pete, they're off," I called out to Ben.

"Can't – he's admitting a patient."

Just then Tom Lewis came in, red in the face, asking for Bobby.

"Haven't seen him to-day sir; have you checked the postroom?"

Ignoring my reply, he asked, "Is that the race I can hear?"

"Coronation Cup sir."

"Yes, someone told me Barnes had some good information, blast him."

The radio filled in the following silence, "Narrator holding on from Darius, wins by a length." Tom disappeared. Ben and I grinned at each other. Two up – one to go!

The third leg of our treble, due off at 4.35, wasn't on the radio, but we had arranged for Bobby to phone us the result. Ben, Pete and I had synchronised watches, following the second hand round.

"Its seven furlongs," I said, "so it'll take about a minute and a half."

Nobody spoke; the rattling of the hospital trolley in the corridor filtered through. After an agonising wait, the phone rang. Ben grabbed it.

"Hello Bobby – it won – 5-1– are you sure – bloody hell – cheers," Ben put down the phone.

"It won – Penthouse won – 5-1 – bloody hell," he repeated to our beaming faces.

I can remember shouting out "Miss Deecie I love you," and looking up to see the Orthopaedic Squadron Leader in the doorway, holding an x-ray up to the light.

"Church do you know the difference between a knee and an elbow?"

"Yes sir."

"No you don't, now sharpen up and get your act together."

Our winnings totalled around £125, and even divided by four, it exceeded our individual net pay for over three months. Our celebration at the Angel Inn however, was marred somewhat by a scuffle between Bobby (five pints of Mackeson and a whisky chaser) and the Station Warrant Officer, Tom Lewis. Tom, furious at being excluded from the syndicate after lending Bobby money in the past, found it hard to witness our rejoicing.

Later that year, Bobby Barnes was mysteriously posted to Renfrewshire.

Churchy's Golden Goose

Betting systems are great when they are successful, and when they win continually, they make dreams come true – that is until the dream becomes a nightmare. And so it was with my year-long posting to Bristol University Air Squadron.

Housed in one of the bleak huts at the far end of Filton Airport, a place where mugs of tea froze in winter, and in summer you were bitten by mosquitoes, the posting had its compensations, for not only was I driven to the centre of Bristol every day to work, but I was also given permission to practice my trumpet.

Ensconced in a converted private house at the back of the University, my duty as a newly promoted Senior Aircraftsman was to look after the records of students learning to fly light aircraft at Filton. The resident staff of an Adjutant, a civilian secretary and myself, was supplemented by two drivers who shuttled the students to Filton.

Since my duties and those of secretary Glenda were very light, I was encouraged by Flight Lieutenant Ruggles, the Adjutant, to turn the lounge into an Air Students' Club, opening a bar and running a pie and tea swindle. In addition, I was asked to purchase the latest long-playing records for the newly-donated radiogram, and a few suitable magazines, such as *Flight*. It was two or three months before *The Sporting Life* and the *Greyhound Express* were added to the list, but added they were!

Due to my stammer, I was inclined to be a loner, spending many evenings with my greyhound papers in front of the stove. On one such evening, my corporal asked why I wasn't over the NAAFI with the other men. I explained that I was working on a new system, using the recent average times of greyhounds when they got a clear run. He seemed to be impressed, and to my surprise gave me a £1 (his day's pay) to cover my selections the next time I went racing.

Bristol then had two dog tracks – Knowle, a small out-of-town track that raced on Wednesday nights and Saturday afternoons, and Eastville, then the home of Bristol Rovers, where they raced on Tuesday and Friday evenings. Very soon I was attending all the meetings, and by using a staking plan to cover my selections, hoped to make a profit, stopping at a winner.

The system was an instant success and Corporal Buchan was paid out £6 after the first three weeks. Although the 'dividends' from each meeting were small, they were constant, and as yet there had been no losing meetings.

Very soon, through Corporal Buchan's free publicity, I had more than a dozen Airmen giving me money to bet for them. This I agreed to do, on condition my expenses were taken out of the pool and that dividends were paid out once a month. After a further two months of continued success, I upped the ante by asking for 10% of the payout. No one objected. Eventually my two drivers, who were by now both part of the syndicate, leaked the news of *Churchy's Golden Goose* to both Glenda and my Adjutant. At first, Flt-Lt Ruggles said he wasn't in favour of betting, but thought the Government's new Premium Bonds scheme was admirable. Glenda on the other hand, was keen to join, but did not want Ruggles to know about it. That Friday she gave me half her salary as a down payment and, a week later, was at my side at Eastville.

As the syndicate grew, so did the stakes, and my bets regularly affected the starting prices, while the bigger bookmakers granted me bits over the odds. Further benefits followed as the weeks rolled into months. I was now regularly treated to supper in the NAAFI, allowed unofficial extra days' leave – yes, the Adjutant thought he would be part of the fun after all, and even arranged speech therapy for me. Finally, to allow me more time to study the form, the *Greyhound Express* and *The Sporting Life* were ordered for the lounge, the latter because many of the officers thought they could 'earn' even more if I would work on a horseracing system.

Although there were occasional weeks when the prices of our winners would not recoup our total stakes, overall we had nine months of steady success and not once had we gone through the card without a winner. Several of the syndicate thought my system was invincible and drew out their holiday savings to add to their investment, while many others refused to take the dividends, ploughing them back into their stake. Glenda, a pillar of the syndicate's administration, was considering selling some of her husband's shares.

One Friday night, Glenda and I travelled to Eastville in her newly acquired estate car, with a holdall packed with pound notes. Two hours later, after six straight losers, we were £300 down. Needing to compose myself, I decided to skip the seventh race and wait for the last. Our maximum bet of £150 (my weekly wage was £4), was placed by Glenda and I in two hits at 3-1 and 5-2, on Real Treasure – trap three.

The hare rattled past the traps. Suddenly all our concentration was focused on the white jacket, a fast starter. He trapped well and led into the final bend. From then on, Mighty Mo, the deposed favourite in trap one, made steady headway, until the pair passed the post locked together.

"Oh God, what do you think Michael?"

"Never mind about that," I said, "go down and put this on Mo in the photo," and handed her £120 from my reserve kitty.

"Try to get odds against, then we can't lose whichever one wins."

Glenda sped down to the bookies and I saw them take the cash. Just then the Tannoy announced "First trap one, Mighty Mo."

What happened next was to affect the lives of 26 Airmen.

Glenda returned looking like death.

"I've backed the wrong bloody dog," she gasped, "I just can't believe it."

I was speechless. In seconds we had gone from a no-lose situation to a total disaster. On the night we had lost £570.

Later that night, Glenda said she would make good her £120 mistake by selling her car. It was a tough decision, but it quelled the threat of a lynching when I returned to camp.

Over the next week, no-one spoke of anything else – everyone was affected, and immediately all the goodwill vanished. Glenda was given much sympathy, but not from her husband, who, having believed her car was in for repair, saw it for sale in a Bristol showroom. Later that week, he was also forced to query the disappearance of their new refrigerator, which Glenda had also found necessary to sell.

After the immediate anger died down, everyone accepted that *Churchy's Golden Goose* was cooked. But three weeks later some of the syndicate, missing the excitement and the hope it had given them, started to put the loss into perspective. After all, it had only bombed out once in nine months, and if they had not kept ploughing back their winnings they would still be ahead.

Slowly the punters returned, and, at a reunion in the NAAFI, eight of them agreed to continue, but this time amending the increase in stakes between the fifth and seventh selections.

That Saturday afternoon I returned to Knowle, a tight track with an inside hare and trap 6 vacant. Success came quickly, my dog winning the first race, at odds of 4-5. Not great, but we were up and running and, over the next two weeks I notched up successes at six other meetings.

One morning Glenda, and Flt-Lt Ruggles, who had been giving her lifts to and from work, called me up to his office.

"Look Church," he said, staring at his blotting pad, "I think people have said a lot of unfair things about you. After all, it wasn't your fault they bet more money than they could afford to lose. By all accounts its a very fine system and," he paused, looking up, "if it's all right with you, Glenda and I would like to be part of it again."

Minutes later, in the Air Students' lounge, I was pouring out Ruggles's favourite tipple – Amontillado sherry – into three glasses, to toast our future success.

The very next Wednesday evening, I stood high in the stand at

Eastville. It was pouring with rain and by the fourth race puddles began to form at the first bend. Why I had gone along to the Puppy Heats I will never understand. Although all the dogs had had one or two trials over the course and distance, I could never justify their reliability. Inevitably, disaster struck – seven straight losers – a lethal blow to my hopes of becoming a professional punter in civvy street.

The following week, a posting to a Fire Fighting course in Chorley, Lancs, suddenly became expedient. The C.O. coyly explained that it was for my personal protection, allowing me to transfer my kit from Filton to Bristol, while I waited for the date to arrive.

I left with no good-byes, although the duty driver wished me good riddance as I struggled to get my kitbag out of the back of the jeep. My stay at Bristol had been a roller-coaster ride and, as is the way with these things, I had got off at the bottom.

Alone again, while waiting for my train at Temple Meads Station, I suddenly had the germ of an idea, but that's another story!

Another Nail in my Coffin

My return to civvy street after doing two years' National Service was harder for me than most. Having led the life of a professional punter during my stay in the RAF (plus a little trumpeting on the side), to return to the rigours of the Inland Revenue was not easy. I did of course continue to put the PAYE section's bets on at Charlie Young's when I popped out to get their cigarettes or chocolate, but now, qualified and on the staff, I was thought by my superiors to have outgrown this role.

What I did find irksome was being told by the Inspector that, in future, it would be better for my career if I was not seen to take an active part in betting. Unfortunately this directive came at a bad time, since I had just spent £200 on buying a decent greyhound, and his successes, along with my photograph, had appeared in the *Greyhound Express*. Although Charlie Young had read the paper – and that meant that half of Woking knew – I was still under 21, and feared if my bosses found out I would be for the high jump.

A few weeks later, Laddie – alias Suir Shell – sprained a tendon, and my trainer Denis Hannafin thought it more economical for me to keep the dog at home (no galloping allowed), until he fully recovered. Now this in itself was quite a big thing for us. Mum had to cook and mince his food – breasts of lamb, oxhearts, cabbage and rusks – and I had to gently walk him for two or three miles every day.

All went along nicely until, one morning, while walking the dog over the Wheatsheaf Common, I stopped to tie my shoelace, looping the lead over my foot. Suddenly, Laddie saw a rabbit and dived into the bushes. I chased after him, but he had vanished. Twenty minutes later, walking back home across the common, I spotted him waiting for me at the corner of the road, thankfully unharmed. Eventually, I got to work an hour late and my excuse that my Nan had suffered a funny turn was treated with grave suspicion.

From then on, I did my best to keep a low profile, until the day of the Lincolnshire Handicap, when I was asked to draw up the office sweep. Thirty-two runners – two bob a head – pay first, second and third and, since there were more than 32 tickets sold, a few blanks were added. One lunch-time – for this sort of thing could never interrupt the work – I wrote out the list of runners, cutting and folding them into an old tea-caddy. One by one the staff drew out the names, blanks and all. But at the end, one horse had not come out – Babur.

We searched everywhere. George, who drew the first blank, said he should have it. But mysteriously everyone who had paid had drawn out a piece of paper. In the end, rather than let it take over the whole afternoon, it was decided to leave things as they were and hope Babur didn't win. The situation reminded me of the special Tote Lincoln pool a decade earlier, when, according to a member of their staff, the winner – Fair Judgement, I think it was – had been omitted from the thousands of coupons sent out to account holders!

At around 3.15, a few enthusiasts drifted into the filing room, a long narrow office where the two filing clerks, one with a glass eye and one with a wooden leg, were listening to the race on their secreted radio.

"Bloody Babur, who'd have thought it?" said Paddy (the leg).

"Which lucky bugger drew that, Michael?" said Andy (the eye).

As things were, I was unable to answer either question, so I went back to my section leader, Miss Cartwright, for a Revenue ruling.

"It's quite straight forward," she said, looking over my head as if receiving an answer from above.

"The person who drew the second horse gets the second prize and the person who drew the third horse gets the third prize."

"Yes, but who gets the first prize?" I pleaded.

"No one," she responded. "According to you, no one drew the winner."

"But what shall I do with the m-m-money, Miss."

"Church, this is the last straw. It's typical of everything you lay your hands on – one cock-up after another – I thought that you of all people would be able to organise a racing sweep. Put the money in the Barnado's box."

Over the next year, my clerical efficiency record continued to decline, as did my confidence. In fact, the Inspector had such a bulging file of complaints that he would often ask me if there was, perhaps, some other career I would like to pursue. But needing a steady income and not wishing to upset my security-minded parents, I continued to turn up for work.

A year on, two of my uncles, Albert, a fish vendor cum-racing-tipster, and Charlie, reputedly Woking's fastest bricklayer, came to ask if Dad or I wanted to accompany them to Lincoln to see the big race the following Wednesday. Pleased to do so, we concocted our usual excuses, Dad (a bad back) and me (asthma and hayfever – out of season). Mum enjoyed these cloak-and-dagger situations and told them about the previous year's sweep. Putting in my twopennyworth, I added: "Babur was sired by My Babu, the 2,000 Guineas winner, who I named my beautiful pet rabbit after."

All this coincidental but useless information seemed to bamboozle my Uncles, and it took a while to assure Charlie that I was not proposing to take the rabbit with us.

The weather on Lincoln Day was dull, dank and rainy. Dad, ironically, had a bad back on the morning of the race and didn't go; so with my Uncles in the front seats of the fish van, I happily rattled around in the back, like a ping-pong ball in a bucket.

Due to a swirling mist and heavy traffic, we didn't arrive on the racecourse until 20 minutes before the big race. Nicholas Nickleby (Scobie Breasley up), was our unanimous choice, but the incident of the Tax Office Sweep caused both Albert and I, superstitiously, to have a ten-shilling each-way saver on Babur. Carrying over a stone more than last year, Babur, ridden by Edgar Britt, was an exceptionally late foal, and although now five years-old, was still capable of improvement.

Because of the poor visibility, the leaders first came into view about three furlongs out. Who You, one of the light-weights, was in front, but Babur was close up. A furlong out, Britt shook Babur up, and the last 100 yards was pure joy. Albert and I cleared £18 each for our superstition, but poor Charlie came back ranting.

"Some bastard's stolen my wallet – all my wages – over £20."

Albert and I tried to console him. First we told the Police, and then we retraced his steps on the chance that he might have dropped it, but all to no avail. Finally, Albert and I offered to make it up out of our winnings, but, being a very proud man, Charlie refused to take it as a gift, saying he would be pleased to borrow £10 for the week.

That night, knowing that Laddie was running at Wimbledon, the Uncles and I agreed, (as was usually the case when I was in their company), that we would play up our winnings – or in Charlie's case, losings – on the dogs.

Thanks to some determined driving by Albert, we turned into the Plough Lane track with ten minutes to spare. In these pre-seeding days, Suir Shell had been entered two day's previously as a reserve, and although a railer, had taken the place of the lame dog in trap six. I explained to the Uncles that in the light of the draw, the 100-7 on offer reflected his chance and it was very likely he would be bumped off the track. In spite of this and in view of our long journey, we trusted to luck; Albert and I had ten bob each-way on him on the Tote, while Charlie disappeared to queue elsewhere, until finally, we all met up near the traps.

As the hare approached, I could see Laddie crouching down, eagerly watching the rail. Suddenly the traps sprung, he flew out and, leading two lengths into the first bend, he crossed over to the rails. Down the back straight he maintained a length lead until the final bend, where he was joined by traps one and four. From where we stood it was impossible to tell if he'd won, but the Tannoy informed us "Photograph, photograph." We waited.

"First trap six, Suir Shell, second trap one, Cregane Surprise."

"Thank heavens for that," said Charlie.

"Well done Michael," Albert said beaming.

"Gosh, he d-deserved that d-didn't he," I gasped, beginning to shake.

"Where do I cash these?" said Charlie, showing Albert his tickets.

"Bloody hell Charlie, this looks good, one-two-three forecast tickets on six and one."

We strode off to the payout windows. Albert and I had done well enough, but Charlie was paid out £24.

Unfortunately, George from the tax office was also in the payout queue. He had never really forgiven me for the sweep cock-up the previous year, and I knew that reports of my bogus hayfever would inevitably prove to be another nail in my coffin. But what the hell, my dog was brilliant, and later, holding pints of ale, laughing and slapping each other on the back, we felt like 'The Three Musketeers'.

Glorious Goodwood

Alf was carefully chalking the numbers from one to 36 around the front tyre of the coach. This was Stewards' Cup day, and for many the 'sweep on the wheel' would be their first bet of the day. The coach trip to 'Glorious Goodwood,' run by our local working mens' club, was always fully booked and many of the stalwarts on board had been saving for this day since Christmas.

This year, I had been assigned by Mum as 'guide for the day' to Martha and Bucky, distant friends over from Dayton, Ohio. Keen racegoers in the States, they were eager to sample the delights of an English race meeting. However, by choosing a working mens' club outing, they were about to be exposed to the primitive delights peculiar to that genre.

Five miles out of Woking, Alf, the senior bar steward, was joyfully handing out bottles of pale ale, Bass and Worthington for the men, and miniature bottles of spirits for the ladies. Having got everyone loosened up, he then went round collecting two shillings a head for the numbers on the wheel, (each passenger being allotted the number on their seat), and the same amount for the traditional Stewards' Cup sweep.

Alf, by this time, pleased with the smooth running of the business end of things, generously assisted my bookmaking ambitions by announcing, "If any of you are going to have small each-way bets, I suggest you give them to young Michael, as they probably won't take them on the course."

Our first stop for 'refreshments' was the Half Moon in Petworth. Everyone was keen to stretch their legs, and it was 'getting to know you' time as the passengers mingled. Alec and Danny, two 'likely lads,' certainly used the time well, chatting up the Littlewood sisters, Wendy and Maureen. Meanwhile, having collected about a dozen small bets, I kept a distant eye on Bucky and Martha, unsuccessful in their quest for either Root Beer or Daiquiris. They had been cornered by Smithy, an expert on the Turf, but badly handicapped with pebble glasses and two walking sticks.

"Back on the bus folks, or we'll never get there," Alf pleaded, and slowly the pints were emptied and the seats were filled. Traffic was now building up alarmingly and in the next half-hour the passengers' bladders reached capacity. Even Martha and Bucky politely enquired about the next washroom facilities. As we were then stationary, Stan, our driver, decided to follow the example of the coaches ahead and release the passengers to take their chances in the hedgerows. Gents to the right, Ladies to the left, seemed to be the etiquette. Although the more discreet ladies could be observed laughing and stumbling towards the privacy of a distant thicket.

Eventually everybody returned, some more dishevelled than others but, after another round of bottled beers, including a Bass for the driver, any inhibition that lingered was swept away, as the volume of noise and laughter rose by a hatfull of decibels. 'No Limit Banker' was in full swing across the back seat, and a four-handed game of Spoof (three matches per hand), stretched across the gangway. Martha and Bucky, who by necessity had taken advantage of the hedgerow washroom, watched in awe as the Littlewood sisters got down to some serious snogging with Alec and Danny. Such was everyone's preoccupation, that no-one (except the driver, of course), noticed us turn into the racecourse. Journeying along from the straight six furlong start, we lined up with 30 or 40 other coaches.

In time-honoured tradition, Stan the driver was first out of the coach and, checking for the winning number on the front tyre, let forth a stream of expletives. Soon passengers were pressing in on all sides.

"What's the winning number," Bucky enquired.

"I wish I bloody knew," replied Stan, "someone must have peed over the wheel at the Half Moon!"

Alf, well trained in thinking on his feet, instantly came up with a solution.

"The money on the wheel goes into the big race sweep – that should double the winner's prize."

Moments later, Alf, small but with Sampson like strength, was sliding out trestle tables from the under-carriage of the coach, assisted by a number of glazed but willing helpers. And while the ladies spread out table-cloths and covered them with all manner of meat pies, sausage rolls and sandwiches, Alf, now having enlisted the assistance of Bucky and I, distributed a full bottle of spirits to each of the passengers. According to Alf, this was all in the price, thanks to the generosity of the Committee.

A pork pie, two radishes and a glass of neat gin was not my usual diet for picking winners, but half-way down the gin bottles and well before the first race, most of our party were confident that it was going to be their lucky day. Even Martha, who had managed to dilute her vodka with a Pepsi, had suddenly become psychic.

"Today the Smiths have it," she said. "I've been talking to Smithy of the pebble glasses; I think it's an omen. He was telling me about the Smith brothers, Doug and Eph; said they were the jockeys to follow."

Bucky preferred to bet on the names, and being in England, fancied Queensberry and Tudor Monarch, the latter particularly, since it was owned and bred by Sir Winston Churchill.

I proudly guided my middle-American charges up to Trundle Hill, where they admired the view, but had to admit they had never watched racing from so far away. Lending them my binoculars went some way to placating them but, after Doug Smith won the first race and brother Eph the second on Queensberry, they seemed to be settling in nicely.

Next up was the Stewards' Cup – 21 runners and the biggest betting race of the meeting. Bucky, looking to play up his winnings on Churchill's Tudor Monarch, and Martha, convinced of the infallibility of the Smith brothers, headed off to the Tote, taking with them my ten-bob each-way Deer Leap.

Trying to call a race head-on from about a mile away is almost impossible, but halfway up the straight, I could see Manny Mercer on Deer Leap heading affairs. Into the final furlong, he was still well clear and I was counting my money when suddenly, the pink, chocolate sleeves and cap of Tudor Monarch came out of the pack to challenge. Could Mercer hold on? Bucky hoped not, and he was right. The Tannoy announcement wavered across the downs, "First Tudor Monarch 25-1, second Deer Leap 22-1, third St Elmo 100-8." The Yanks were delighted and I was more than pleased with my 10-1 place odds on Deer Leap.

Throughout the afternoon, Martha had been obsessed with the bookmakers and tic-tac men, and although her profits had been dented by Lester Piggott winning the next two races, she desperately wanted to bet with a bookie before returning home. Naturally it had to be on a Smith.

Doug was riding the Boyd-Rochfort two-year-old Jet Stream.

"That's the one," Martha said, pressing a pound in my hand. Bucky wanted the same and gave me another pound, adding, "Do your best Michael; we'll come and watch."

Bookmakers on Trundle Hill weren't usually known for their wild generosity, but amongst all the 7-2's I spotted a 4-1 and dived in.

"Ten quid to collect if you win," I told them.

Giving them a commentary on the race was a pleasure – Jet Stream led from tape to line. And Martha, given the ticket to collect the dough, made much play with the ten one pound notes, laughing and waving them around.

Battling back through the crowds to find our coach, Martha and Bucky, eager to tell the tale of their success, rejoined their fellow travellers who, now in a more laid-back mood, had formed a large, seated circle on the grass. Predictably, about a dozen of them had not moved from the coach all afternoon, and were now more laid out than laid back.

Robert, the assistant bar steward, check waistcoat and beret, was serenading the circle with his accordion, and two gypsy women who had gate-crashed the party were, in the absence of tea leaves, reading palms. And while Martha and Smithy were recounting the success of his namesakes, I retrieved our three partially filled bottles of spirits.

One 'drunk as a skunk' Turfite from another coach staggered into our circle. His binoculars had swung around to the middle of his back and appeared to balance his equilibrium, for, after having taken three steps forward, the weight of his bins contrived to drag him back. Soon it was obvious to everyone that he was going to fall, but which way? Thinking quickly I borrowed Smithy's walking sticks and crossing them in the centre of the circle to give us north, south, east and west, I encouraged the punters to bet on which way he would fall. The 2-1 odds I offered were not, in truth, for their benefit, but the entertainment value was great. Every time he tottered north, folk

127

would shout across their bets and throw over their cash. Then, when he staggered back, they would call out south and throw over more money for me to record. Since his shambling progress continued for nearly five minutes, a small crowd had gathered to watch the fun, and my take on the event would have been the envy of any bookmaker on Trundle Hill. Just when we thought he might stagger out of the circle, he went down to a great cheer. After close inspection, it was agreed he was inclined east, a very good result for me.

Climbing aboard the coach, we learnt that Alf had won the double sweep, but was in no fit state to receive this news or any other, as he was out cold, having been aided back to his seat by conscientious family members. Looking around, I noticed that the Littlewood sisters, whose pettycoats and beehive hairdo's were looking more than a little distressed, had changed partners with Danny and Alec. Meanwhile, those who still had a little money and were conscious, continued with the 'No Limit Banker' and rounds of Spoof. Feeling queasy, but otherwise contented, I settled down to count my day's profit, but was soon disturbed by angry voices a few seats behind. Looking around, I saw two chaps, both very much the worse for wear, taking poorly aimed swings at each other. This continued for a short time until they both simultaneously passed-out and keeled over onto the seats, where they snored happily for the rest of the journey.

As we pulled into the Crown for the use of their toilets, Stan shouted out,

"Fifteen minutes only, if you're not back I'm going without you." Thirty minutes later, he went in to dig them out, but by then most people could not have told you who they were, let alone how long they had been there. Eventually, just as Stan was shepherding a few stragglers back on the bus, those aboard, having become restless, were going in for the second shift. This pantomime continued for some time with most of those passing to and from the pub breaking into impromptu dances on route, Martha and Bucky executing a very well-received square dance.

Eventually, all were aboard, and everyone agreed that Stan had 'been a brick' by not driving off without us. So, rather than ask him to do the usual, slow, one-by-one, drop-off routine, we all agreed to go back to the club, tipping generously when the hat was taken round on his behalf.

Tumbling out of the coach to the church clock striking 12, we were still a very rowdy bunch; many had now got their second wind and were determined to sing their way to their doorsteps. Martha and Bucky thanked me, in song, for my company and then slowly wended their way along Church Street, harmonising their own particular version of 'Show Me the Way to Go Home'.

If I could have had one last bet that day, it would have been that Martha and Bucky would never, ever, have a day's racing quite like that again.

The Demon King

"Lot 127 – Timber King – a black dog from County Cork – 20 months old – just two trials at Youghal – who'll start me off at 20 guineas?"

Silence followed.

"Last trial, clocked a useful 31.55 on .40 slow, when second at Youghal. A big, strong dog for his age," pleaded the auctioneer.

At last a hand went up at the back.

"Twenty guineas, thank you sir, who'll give me 25?"

Nervously I waved my programme.

"Twenty five on my right. Thirty to you at the back sir? No? Anyone else ?"

The hammer fell.

"Sold to the young gent on my right."

Within seconds I had signed the chitty and paid in cash. And it wasn't until I was given the greyhound's identity book that I realised I had bought the wrong dog!

Freddie, a mate of mine, had driven me up to Aldridges Greyhound Sales, near Euston, for although I had owned greyhounds before – and the last, a top grader at Wimbledon – I thought it would be fun to own and train a dog at a nearby flapping track.

I'd had the catalogue for three weeks, and spent many happy hours assessing the greyhounds on sale, pencilling in what I thought they would go for. But all to no avail since, although we had got there early and examined the dogs, I thought I was bidding for the faster litter brother, who not only shared the same pen but looked almost identical. Worse was to come; after clearing up his mess in the back of Freddie's van, a closer inspection revealed fleas, worms and mange.

A month of powders, potions and injections, interspersed with lashings of TCP followed, before we finally got him to Aldershot for his grading trials. The first Sunday he had a 275-yard, three-dog-trial and finished second. The next trial that day was made memorable by a young dog running so wide that he disappeared under the spectator rail, to re-emerge half-way up the terracing, eventually re-joining the track just before the winning post. The following Sunday, our dog looked much sharper, running on to win a 500-yard four-dog-trial in 29.30 secs. Freddie and I were ecstatic, but an official in the control tower came rushing down to ask us not to blab it around as it would spoil the price! Having been used to NGRC tracks, I could not understand his concern, until the following Friday. Running in the third race and re-named Tar Baby, our pride and joy had been given a grading time of 29.80 (50 spots slower), and had drawn trap six.

Brimming with hope, we had brought friends and family to see the race and had borrowed a large van for the night, which also accommodated Timber King – alias Tar Baby – pet name Skippy.

On arrival, the charms of the flapping track were instantly apparent. Clandestine family groups formed huddles on the terraces, each huddle believing it knew something the other huddles didn't. When a race was in progress, future runners, pulling and frantically barking on the sidelines, were sometimes restrained from joining in by children smaller than the dogs. Occasionally a dog got loose on the track, so voiding the race. Very occasionally this was used as a ploy to avert an impending, disastrous loss. Despite all this, there was an underlying friendliness in the people, who held a passionate love for their dogs.

To add to the fun, the place was seething with colourful characters. Before our race, one authoritative group member, seeing our party to be newcomers, came over to wise us up on which dogs on the card 'weren't off'. However, his get-rich information was somewhat undermined by the string keeping up his trousers.

As was usual at flapping tracks, the bookmakers were very cautious, offering around 2-1 against each of the six runners. Freddie and my father, Stan, held our stakes and the general opinion was to play late. This we discovered was a big mistake. For while I was parading the dog, a Frankensteinian figure of a man, dressed in a black hat and black cloak with a scarlet lining, whirled up and down the line of bookmakers betting £50 a time on our dog, until the price fell to evens. When Freddie and I caught sight of him, we thought he bore a marked resemblance to the man in the control tower the previous Sunday. Forever after, he was known to us as 'The Demon King'.

Slipping Skippy into his trap, I ran back to the pick-up point at the end of the home straight. The hare, a rugby football with a tail of trailing polythene and driven by an upturned motorbike, whizzed past the traps. Skippy was slowly away but, after moving into third place at the first bend, he barged his way through down the back straight to lead into the third bend. Here the track had two levels; the inside being six inches or so lower, while the outside banked up to a foot or more higher. From the stand this gave Skippy the appearance of being on stilts for about 20 yards, and also gave the railers a chance to get back at him. But around the final bend, he found an extra gear and pulled away, with family, friends and myself, leaping up and

down and shouting for joy. The winning time was announced as 28.90 secs, 40 spots faster than his trial, but 90 spots faster than the racecard. There was no stewards' inquiry for time-finding, thankfully, and when I quizzed an official on how 29.30 had become 29.80, he replied, "Must have been a typing error; we get them sometimes. Still, you're not complaining are you?"

Re-united with our gang in the cafeteria, we shared out our modest winnings – £25 at even-money! It was a lesson well-learned on 'getting on', especially as there was no prize money and owners paid to get in. For all that, it was a most happy and memorable occasion.

Skippy was a regular at Aldershot for just over a year and, like most graders he won in his turn, although he and I did endure a run of seven consecutive seconds, including one night when the orange and red balls used for making the trap draw were surprisingly mixed up and we were given trap one, as a wide runner!

Feeding dogs at this time was entirely different from now, for these were pre-Pedigree Chum days. A typical meal was made up of breast of lamb or ox heart, cabbage, onions and potatoes, most of which went through a mincing machine, before being boiled vigorously. The pungent odour permeated every corner of the house, and every article of clothing. The race-day menu was easier, with a preparation of two slices of toast, two raw eggs and half a glass of sherry.

As time went by, friends and family supported less and less, and as a non-driver, many is the time I caught the train from Woking to Aldershot with Skippy and then walked two miles to the track. After racing, the return trip rarely got us home before midnight. Unfortunately this, together with a five-mile-a-day walking regime, began to impinge on my budding sex life. Nevertheless, it was fun.

Slowly, other commitments began to creep into my life. Two or three nights a week I played the trumpet in a modern jazz group, and a must-see girl named Pat was making regular appearances in my diary. One evening a local bookie made me an offer for the dog and I let him go.

The following spring, while eating my sandwiches in the park, a newspaper, caught by the wind, wrapped itself around my legs. As I leant to gather it up, my trained eye was drawn to the greyhound results from Wandsworth the night before. And there it was, yes, you've guessed it, *1st Timber King 7-4 favourite.* The old boy had the last laugh, winning a top-grade stayers' event at a pukka track. How nice!

St Paddy and St Peter's

Seldom have these two Saint's names been linked outside the church. But for this Church, and in this yarn, they are forever entwined.

Unable to survive on the proceeds from my jazz trumpeting, I took the job of statistician with Kenwood's – a local company who made foodmixers. Fortunately for me, my boss, Ron Noble (a handsome, larger than life character) was a racing man and, adopting the maxim of hitching your wagon to a star, as he progressed in the company, I followed. After about six months, Ron was promoted to UK Sales Chief and I was given the task of setting targets, organising sales competitions and getting Ron's bets on.

Ron's favourite punt was a five-shilling each-way treble, and in the time that I knew him, he brought off some spectacular wins. On one occasion, after the first two legs had gone in at 8-1 and 10-1, I telephoned him during an important Sales meeting to give him 'the progress report', and to enquire if he wanted to hedge off on the third leg. Without blowing the gaff, he replied, "Glad to hear my proposal is bearing fruit and I am confident about the original forecast."

The morning price on his third selection was 6-4, so Ron's

confidence appeared well placed, but what he didn't know was that, by throwing his jockey and bolting halfway round the course, the horses's price had drifted to 100-8. Still, just to prove that miracles do happen, it won easily. Later that afternoon, I went into his office to give him the good news.

"Super, well done, how much have I won?" Ron was then on about £30 a week and I on £12,

"Three hundred and fifty-t-two quid," I stammered.

The following day, after providing me with an 'armed guard' from the bookies, he generously put £25 in my pocket.

That September, on a day's racing at Ascot, I was impressed with the smooth victory of St Paddy in the Royal Lodge Stakes. A son of Aureole, out of a Bois Roussel mare, he looked to have all the right credentials for next year's Derby. So, from almost every pay packet afterwards, I would take out a few shillings and send a postal order to William Hill, backing St Paddy for the Derby.

The Kenwood Christmas do that year was held over to January. UK Sales had been outstanding and, after the usual speeches, Ron gave out prizes to the top salesmen. Since I had heard that a modern band had been booked for the night, I brought my trumpet along and sat in on a couple of numbers. Fortunately Pat, my teenage girlfriend, was impressed and I got a lift back to her place on her Lambretta scooter.

Pushing my luck the following day, I asked her if I could have a go at driving – a reckless idea, since I had difficulty riding a bike, and to this day have never learned to drive a car! However, against Pat's better judgement, with as much brandy in my veins as blood, and worse still, with no insurance, I zoomed off without a care in the world. Approaching a crossroads, while attempting to read a sign post, I neglected to slow down. Fortunately Pat was thrown clear, but I, wouldn't you know it, was unable to move from under the scooter and, despite my protests to the Ambulance man that I had to get to Sandown Park in an hour, I was carted off to St Peter's Hospital, Chertsey, with a broken hip. That evening I re-awoke to find my leg in traction and as plastered as I had been.

Six weeks can be a long time in bed, but the special delivery of *The Sporting Life*, *Greyhound Express* and *Racing and Football Outlook*, via the daily visit of the hospital's bookie's runner, kept up my interest. Quaintly, as a recreational therapy, I was encouraged to make a toy horse from felt, wire and stuffing. I made him in the Sassoon colours of blue and yellow hoops and called him St Paddy. Ron Noble was a constant visitor, bringing in both fruit and Sales targets for revision. Later, I was swamped with 100 get well cards after his memo to all Sales reps also bore fruit. It was at this time that I invented the 'Kenwood Wheel' – a natty gizmo designed to show product savings at the flick of a finger.

Throughout my incarceration, Pat also visited me every day and sometimes at night, passing letters and presents through the bedside window. Rather than dwell on my sexual frustrations, I found a new passion – Chess!

Paterson Ward was always well stocked with motor-cycle casualties, mostly on traction. Five of these made up the rather grandly named Chess Club. Chess is a slow game by any standards, but here it was made even slower by the necessity of orderlies, nurses and the occasional doctor having to pass the board across the ward.

Being a novice, I was a prime target for 'fools mate'. However, on my last morning, I recorded my first victory – a sweet, two-rook scissor movement – against an Austrian called Fritz. He was furious and immediately wanted a replay. Fortunately for me the transport was waiting to take me home, and I was able to take my leave, still in plaster but flushed with success.

My early return to Kenwood's brought both sympathy and

amusement, as unbelievably, Pat ferried me to and fro on the back of the Lambretta – plaster, crutches, briefcase and all.

A few weeks later, we appeared in Court to face the consequences of my driving folly. Pat was fined £100 and disqualified for six months, and I was banned from applying for a licence for two years. But her love and loyalty were such that, come Derby Day, we both set off on bicycles for the 15-mile journey to Epsom Downs.

For those who like a happy ending, St Paddy, assisted by the young Lester Piggott, won the Derby by three lengths, handsomely repaying all those postal order bets I had sent off to William Hill, and providing Pat and I with a three-week camping holiday in the South of France.

Shooting Craps on the 8.27

Around 1961, there was a quartet of commuters who passed the journey from Portsmouth to London Waterloo, by shooting craps. For the uninitiated, craps is a popular American casino game, played with two dice. Briefly, to win, the shooter has to roll a seven or 11 on the first throw. If unsuccessful, he has to throw the number he rolled the first time again, before he throws another seven. The shooter looses if a two, three or 12 appear on the first throw (this is known as craps), or a seven thereafter. Simple isn't it?

Of course there are variations and side bets. In our travellers' case, the players took turns to act as the banker or bookie for the journey, while the other three bet on the game. The original bets are at evens, but if the shooter doesn't win on his first throw, various odds are laid that he will throw the original number before a seven. For those still with us, or for those who have read the first paragraphs for the third time and now think they have a vague understanding of the game, I can now introduce you to the quartet.

Chris, an overweight accountant, would sit in the corner by the window, his shirt sleeves rolled up, forehead slightly sweating whatever the weather, 20 Rothmans and Ronson lighter to hand. Fair Enough Smith, or to his intimates, Smithy, had acquired his handle by repeatedly saying "Fair enough" after almost everything said to him. Also a smoker, he had the worrying habit of laughing and coughing at the same time.

The third member of the quartet was Joyce, an S.P. Settler who worked with Smithy and appeared to be slightly more than a close friend of his. Unfortunately, she had one blue tooth, which showed when she laughed and sometimes stopped others from laughing when they saw it. Finally, Monty was a short, dark, dapper man in his late 50s, now a messenger in the City, but reputedly an ex-member of a Brighton race-gang after the war. Oh yes, I boarded the train at Woking, and on Monty's invitation (I'd met him a couple of times at White City) sat or stood as near as possible to the action. When one of the players was absent, I was invited to play.

On this particularly Friday, as the train rattled through Vauxhall Station, Monty pushed the dice across the table.

"Your roll Chris – I can double the limit for you as it's the last roll today."

"Yeah fine," said Chris who, after vigorously cleaning his glasses, made the pretext of searching through his wallet.

"Can you lend me a fiver until tonight Monty?"

Monty nodded and Chris rolled – "Three – craps – oh shit," Chris groaned as he slumped back in his seat.

Passengers began reaching up into the luggage racks for their coats and briefcases as the train pulled into Waterloo. Soon, hundreds of commuters spilled out onto the platform, but not Chris. Looking dazed, he lingered, lit yet another cigarette and fumbled through his briefcase. A respected £1,000-a-year accountant, Chris had told us he lived with his elderly mother in a big house near Fratton. Lately, however, even I had noticed his losses were getting to him.

The following Monday morning, I located their carriage.

"No Chris?" I enquired hopefully, seeing the vacant seat.

"He's gone to the loo," Monty said, adding, "his luck today is diabolical."

Smithy and Joyce urged Monty to restart the game, but Monty said he would wait and put the dice into his shirt pocket. As the train sped on, they talked of racing and football, until Monty said "You might as well sit in Churchy; it looks as if Chris is involved in another sort of crap game!"

Doubling up on three straight sevens, my shouts of delight drew the attention of other passengers away from their newspapers, adding fuel to my ambition to be a regular in this corner seat.

"Who let Churchy in this game," said Joyce, flashing her tooth.

Just then Chris appeared, "Gyppy tummy," he said sheepishly.

"I see Churchy's getting stuck in. No, no, that's OK, I'll watch. We're nearly there now anyway."

Chris waved his hand to brush aside my offer of his usual seat, looking slightly relieved.

On Tuesday morning, I made my way to the quartet's carriage.

"Chris in the loo?" I asked seeing his place vacant.

"No, he's not with us. Sit in if you like," said Monty.

"Yes, that's fair enough," said Smithy, stifling what was either a laugh or a cough, or both.

Once again I was a few pounds up on the trip, and the following day, with still no sign of Chris, I made a strong finish as the new shooter, after Monty had nearly wiped me out before Clapham Junction.

Before we left the train, Joyce, who had been noticeably quiet throughout the journey, said she would look up Chris's address and Smithy added, "We'll try and phone him – see what's happening."

Next day, hoping to add to my run of luck, I watched the windows of the 8.27 as it arrived at Woking and, catching a glimpse of Monty, hurried along the platform to join him.

"How's Chris?" I said, seeing he wasn't there and eagerly moving across into his place. Looking down at the table, Joyce said, "He's dead. He died late Friday night, after coming back from the pub. Heart, I believe. His big house was really a small flat that he shared with his mum. And she's worried stiff. He hadn't paid the rent for three months and the landlord's been threatening to throw them out."

I looked across at Smithy's black tie.

"Fair enough, I suppose," he said, "but a bit harsh, wouldn't you say?" Joyce started to cry.

"There, there," said Monty, leaning across to comfort her.

"I tell you what," he added, taking three dice out of his shirt pocket, "as a mark of respect, we won't be needing these again," and, reaching up to the window, he hurled the dice out onto the track.

"Why three dice Monty," I asked irreverently,

"Always carry a spare Churchy."

"Fair enough," said Smithy, "but I'd never seen the third dice before."

Throughout the day and that evening, I could think of nothing but Monty's third dice. Next morning, resolving to get into the office a little earlier, I caught the 8.05.

The Levy Board Experience

It was snowing big flakes as I walked down Oxford Street in search of a job. I had been unemployed for three days and was looking for the Brook Street Bureau. Shortly after being told, "It's about 20 yards along on your right," I spotted a pound note on the ground, trodden into the snow. Picking it up by the Bureau entrance, I went inside, hoping to play up my luck.

It seemed that the newly-formed Horserace Betting Levy Board were in need of clerks who were good at maths, knew a bit about racing and had preferably worked for the Government.

Filling in the details of my stay with the Inland Revenue, I gladly put their minds at ease over the other two requirements. And so it was at the HBLB's Euston Road offices later that afternoon where thankfully my knowledge of racing and taxing the public swung it over applicants from Agriculture and Fisheries and the Forestry Commission. In fact, I fell on my feet for, after the first month, I was given a rise and put in charge of the Assessments Division. This, after the legalisation of Betting Shops (May 1, 1961), entailed assessing and collecting monies from bookmakers and the Tote, for the purpose of improving the panorama of horseracing.

The staff, after a couple of months of recruiting, roughly fell into three categories: ex-army personnel, their daughters, and ex-civil servants. For a while, the daughters (rarefied breeds), were allowed to keep their pet dogs (rarefied breeds), under their desks, and this perk seemed to catch on, until dogs of different persuasions confronted each other. Then the posturing, growling and barking would inevitably bring their owners into the fray in an attempt to separate their charges. However, these 'teething problems' were soon sorted, when both 'Pekes' and perks were withdrawn.

It didn't take me long to discover I was the only member of staff with a Secondary Modern education, and there were times when I was more than a little embarrassed, although a few of my colleagues also came from unlikely backgrounds. Gerry, who had studied to be a Cistercian monk in Ireland, was unable to keep silent either then or now, and was famous for phrases such as "I have it backed, sure I have, sure I have." Then there were the two Hugh's – 'Hugh the cash', who was the chief cashier, and 'Hugh the books', who kept track of the 'non-payments'. Both were brought up in the village of Bedgellert, in darkest Wales, and in times of high excitement, reverted to their mother tongue.

At the time, everyone shared a great enthusiasm for the work, but none more than Dennis, who would make the return trip to Angmering in Sussex every day on a moped, having first purchased *The Sporting Life* at 6 am. Then there was Anne, a voluptuous young lady who, in the process of calculating horse transport allowances, was often to be found lying in the middle of the floor on a huge map of Britain, inviting passers by to come down and help her find the way from Bridgwater to Bogside.

Another lady who left a vivid impression was the formidable Miss Hardcastle, a forerunner of Ann Robinson, who, peering over her spectacles, would discharge a volley of cutting remarks that would bring a Brigadier to his knees.

Of course, harnessing these diverse personalities was sometimes a headache, but I had no difficulty in organising the daily Naps Table, encouraged by the hierarchy "to spread a wider understanding of the sport among the staff." This unfortunately they lived to regret, for its inroads into the workload were significant, firstly because of the deliberation over the selections, secondly because of the necessity of keeping the master sheet up-to-date, with all its pluses, minuses and disputes, and finally, the collection of money each week, all of which left very little time to fit in the work. However, it did generate a lot of fun and a nail-biting finish on the final day, with Dennis, myself and Gerry leading at different times in the afternoon, and Gerry celebrating his last race triumph with an exuberant Irish jig on the top of his desk.

A few weeks later, on December 21, 1962, there began a spate of bad weather known as 'The Big Freeze'. Only one race meeting took place (Ayr, January 5), before racing resumed on March 8, and the effect on both betting shops and the Levy Board was devastating.

Now, with the bookmakers' payments down to a trickle, and the staff left in a void after a well-timed directive to close the Naps competition, we could find little or nothing to turn our hands to. That was until the creative activities took over!

To begin with, there was pool betting on the first word uttered by the tea-lady as she entered our office with her trolley, but since she had a colourful vocabulary, there were many rollovers. However, this was such a success that an afternoon version was added. I'm sure the poor woman often wondered why her opening greetings were met with such mixed reactions from the staff.

Then of course, there was the paper dart in the hat game, paying even-money at three paces. Another stimulating challenge was betting on the number of minutes between red buses stopping outside St Pancras Church. This activity kept the two Hughs happily occupied

at their window desks for the best part of the afternoon, and could surely be claimed as the forerunner of spread betting.

The usual diversions such as Pontoon, Poker Dice and Totopoly were, for reasons of decorum, played in our extended lunch break, whilst some of the more restless of the staff would prefer to catch a cab to a nearby Palais, to improve upon their 'Twisting' or to learn the 'Locomotion'. And so it was that many happy hours were productively spent throughout that winter.

Sadly, all this came to an end when racing resumed; that is until Gerry devised a novel Grand National competition. As soon as the weights were published, he encouraged each person to put a cross against their fancy and put two shillings in the kitty. This was repeated every week until the big race, when the horse with the most crosses carried all the money in one huge, each-way bet. Gerry's Cistercian logic was that if we were lucky, we could all celebrate together. Anyway, despite all that, Gerry let the ladies persuade him to divide the kitty between the top two horses. Thus it was that we went down to the bookies with our crock of gold and backed Frenchman's Cove and Mr What.

Leaving a friend's wedding early to watch the race on Mum's TV, a mile and a half's walk away, I was grateful to those cautious ladies, as Frenchman's Cove, our first choice, was brought down, while Mr What finished third at 22-1 behind Kilmore.

Throughout this year and the next, for various reasons, the Levy collected fell short of expectations, and I was gently persuaded to move on. My fond memories of this happy time have now mingled with the reflection that I was possibly not quite mature enough for the job!

Like Father, like Son?

Undoubtedly, one of the biggest influences on my life was that of my father, although as a teenager I would have scorned the suggestion. But, as an only child separated from him during the war, he then took me everywhere, in an effort to make up for lost time. Everywhere there was sport. Horseracing, greyhounds, boxing, speedway, athletics, cycle racing, table tennis, ice hockey, cricket and of course his first love, football.

Football to Dad was watching Woking Football Club, and although I was taken to see Stanley Matthews, Tommy Lawton, Tom Finney and Horatio Carter, such visits were only made when both Woking's first team and their reserves were playing away. I even had to clear the date of my wedding with him lest it coincided with a first team home match, and even then he left half-way through the reception to watch the reserves. So how, why and when did his devotion start?

My Dad Stan's earliest recollection of watching Woking play was in 1910, when, aged five, he climbed through a hole in the fence at the old Pembroke Road ground. Sadly, just before half-time the referee dropped dead, and as a mark of respect, the game was cancelled. In consequence, it was some time before Stan could be convinced that football really was a game of two halves.

All the Church brothers played football for village teams and Stan played right back for Pyrford at the same time as Harry Medhurst, the future Chelsea goalkeeper. But his brother George, actually played for Woking's first team and, as centre-forward, scored on his first appearance.

In the mid 1920's, Good Friday in Woking was celebrated by an all-day six-a-side tournament. The Church brothers entered their own team and often got through a few rounds, although on one occasion they left behind their mascot – a stuffed cat. So superstitious were they that both George and Charlie cycled back home to look for it. Eventually, they found it in the larder but, by the time they returned, their team had been officially scratched and a bye given to their opponents.

Stan served as a gunner in the Royal Artillery during the war, but when home on leave, he would regale me with tales of the Club's success (very little as I remember), although I do recall the names of their international half-back line as A. Cartlidge, E. Payne and T. Briggs.

On his demob, Dad took me to my first home game, during the Christmas holiday of 1945. At the time Oxford City, our opponents, were top of the Isthmian League and Woking were second. A crowd of 4,000 packed into Kingfield and, after a 1-1 draw, Dad and I spent a contented evening going over the game.

The Club's achievements were few and far between in the post-war years until, in 1958, they won the F.A. Amateur Cup at Wembley before a crowd of 71,000, beating Ilford 3-0. Both Stan and I had backed the correct score at odds of 20-1, but we didn't watch the game together. He was proudly seated close to the Royal Box, while I stood with my new girlfriend on the opposite side of the pitch!

Apart from cup-ties, Stan never travelled away, preferring to watch the reserves, but his eccentricities multiplied as he got older when football became his reason for living. On occasions he would take

Mum and I in the Stands, but once, in his excitement, he knocked her off the end seat into the aisle and she never came again. After that, Dad would stand behind the goal, a little left of the net. Here, his anxiety was evident in the flaying elbows that had despatched Mum, and he always cleared a small circle around him. Even if Woking were 4-0 up with three minutes to play, he would be totally unable to enjoy it, desperately whistling at the referee for time.

Once, when my brother-in-law was visiting from Vancouver after an absence of some 15 years, we took him along to the match. Stan found it very puzzling that he was not in England primarily to see the game and found it even harder to comprehend that the poor chap had missed not only last week's cup-tie against Barrow, but would also miss the next important league fixture.

After my mother died, Stan acquired a young Lurcher (Sam) from the local RSPCA dog's home. On Saturdays, both would stand behind the goal, bedecked in red and white scarves. Sam, like most Lurchers, took on the feelings of his master, and would whirl around chasing his tail if Woking scored, only to crouch down behind Stan if the opponents equalised. At half-time, Sam perfected the trick of standing on his hind legs in front of the lads eating beefburgers. He was often rewarded with a piece, but was not above neatly flipping up any unguarded bun to snatch the meat and leave his victim the empty bun. Once, when scolded for this feat by a lad's mother, he reciprocated by peeing in her carrier bag. All the same, as football hooligans go, he was very popular.

Stan could not bear Woking being beaten at home, and, although it happened frequently, he never got used to it. If they were losing particularly badly, rather than soak up any more pain, he would go home and stand in his front garden to hear the shouts of the crowd, if they scored. However, after leaving the ground on one occasion when they were 3-0 down to Leytonstone, he suffered first confusion,

and then embarrassment for, whilst walking away, a series of shouts and cheers seemed to follow him down the road. Finally, unable to control his curiosity, he ran back, and on entering the stadium heard another roar. Returning to his place, he anxiously enquired the score.

"We're 4-3 up Stan; where the bloody hell have you been?"

In later years, Stan would spend Sundays with us, but he would not take his coat off until we had heard his blow-by-blow version of the match. As our family's interest began to wane, so his accounts of the games became more and more exaggerated, until one Sunday he told us, "It was the best game I've ever seen in my life; end-to-end stuff – a real thriller."

"That's encouraging," I responded, "what was the score?"

"Nil-Nil," he said earnestly.

Saturday, May 6, 1989, was 2,000 Guineas day. Shaun (my eldest son) and I went to Newmarket to see Nashwan win in fine style. On our way home we dropped into St Peter's Hospital where dad was being treated for a shadow on his lung. After his polite enquiries about the racing, he asked us the Woking result. This was a home game against Lewes, which, if they won, would promote them back to the Isthmian Premier League. We had tried to find out the score from Newmarket, but it was not until we telephoned from outside the hospital that we learned it was 2-2. We sat in the car outside his ward debating whether or not to tell him, as we knew he would take it badly. Finally we both agreed we had to tell him.

"They drew 2-2 Dad," I said, trying to take away any emphasis from the words. There was a long pause until he said "Well that's it; I've nothing to live for now."

Instinctively, we filled in the silence with "Go on you'll be all right Dad, you'll be there next season;" but he never recovered, and died soon after.

At his funeral, all the wreaths were red and white, and on the way to St Mary's Churchyard, the cortege drove slowly past the football ground. At the next home game he was accorded a minute's silence and a short obituary appeared in the programme.

The following season, our family started to watch Woking again. Stan's dog Sam sported his red and white scarf, and, at the end of the season, appeared on the front cover of the Fanzine as 'Fan of the Year'. Promotion finally came at the end of 1990-91, but before that 'The Cards' had stunned the football world by beating West Bromwich Albion 4-2 at the Hawthorns, and then by going down by a single goal at Everton in the fourth round of the F.A. Cup, taking over 10,000 fans with them for the occasion. Led by their indomitable Manager, Geoff Chapple, further Cup successes followed with three F.A. Trophy victories at Wembley. By now many of us believed Stan was having a word with 'the management above'.

In the season 1996-97, 'The Cards' again reached the third round of the F.A. Cup, after inflicting humiliating defeats on both Millwall and Cambridge. Once again they were featured on *Match of the Day*, this time with a heroic 1-1 draw against Coventry at Highfield Road. By the time the media had proclaimed them the non-league team of the 90s, I had become Club Treasurer, later to be elected their first Commercial Director. Whether Stan had anything to do with all this I do not know, but what I do know is that he would have been very proud of his team – and of his son.

Racing Post and all that

The stories that you have read, and hopefully enjoyed, were the product of a misspent youth, for as a young man I can never remember school or work interfering with the chance of attending a good racemeeting or landing a betting coup. But what happened in the time that followed?

Well, you will be glad to hear that I married Pat, and, after an initial burst of caution, we had four children in five years: Shaun, Sarah, Dominic and Mia. Many years later and just when everyone thought I had become rooted in a local accounting job, I replied to an advertisement for the position of accountant with the *Racing Post* newspaper, weeks before its launch.

Surprised and thrilled to get the job from a number of applicants rivalling the cast of *Ben Hur*, I soon found myself rubbing shoulders with the likes of Sir Peter O'Sullevan and Lord Oaksey and I still remember the first time I shared a urinal with Brough Scott.

Soon after setting up the Accounts systems, my knowledge of horseracing and greyhounds came to the fore, and following an innovative project for the Bloodstock department, and a successful spell as a greyhound 'Spotlight' writer – both 'after hours'– it was obvious where my heart lay.

In what proved to be a crucial transition from accounts to writing my own books, I was appointed to the newly-created post of Special Projects Manager, covering the promotion of racing and greyhound events and *Racing Post* publications. Fortunately for me, successive Editors and Chief Executives – and there were many – allowed me to write a series of classic tomes on bloodlines and the history of the Turf, all of which were successful.

Ripping Gambling Yarns is my first venture into short story writing – I hope it will not be my last.